*This book is not intended a
physicians. The reader shou
relating to their health, parti
require diagnosis or medical

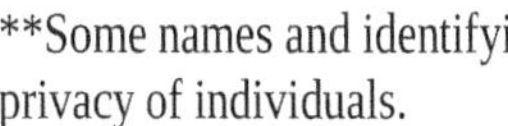

**Some names and identifyi
privacy of individuals.

LEAST RESISTANCE

FOREWORD

I let go of the rope.

it was as simple and as complicated as that.

My hands had been gripped around that rope for most of my life.

Fighting, pulling, dragging … heaving, with every bit of strength I had.

I was exhausted.

On the opposite side of the rope, pulling just as hard, was every unspent emotion I had stored in my body since childhood.

Along with my mother's repressed emotions and her mother's before her and her mother and her mother and so on and so on…

Down through the lineage of my ancestors - shame, guilt, fear, anger … so much anger.

I had been pulling ***against*** those stagnant energies for most of my life, without ever realising it.

Stored in my energetic body were all of the feelings I had ever swallowed down -

and they were heavy, my God, they were heavy:

The shame and guilt I carried over the sexual abuse I suffered, as a ten year old child

The absolute terror I ignored daily - fear that I was different from everyone around me, somehow tainted, dirty and broken.

The constant, low level anxiety over the potential discovery of the fake persona I had created to hide that shame filled ten year old from the world - stoic, tough, no-nonsense, always moving forward.

God forbid anyone should discover the real me, hidden under this suit of armour I had created.

All of those emotions, wrapped up in stories I had been telling myself all my life.

Stories about who I was, who I needed to be and what I needed to do, just to survive in a world of my own perception, that was shaped before I could even talk.

These stories were the silent opponents in a tug of war that I didn't have a snowballs chance in hell of winning.

Until the day I let go of the rope.

And it was in that moment, that I realised I had all the power within me , it had been there all along

But I had been giving that power away by doing one thing over and over again

Resisting reality.

And it was that resistance that was causing the misalignment with who I *truly* am and who I had been presenting to the world. Who I was and who I knew I could be.

This disparity showed up everywhere - in my relationships, in how I mothered my children, in my business ... it was always there, tap tap tapping me on the shoulder.

Like an itch I could not scratch - I had tried, over the years , to distract the itch , of course- I used every distraction technique I could get my hands on - work, wine, sugar, gossip, motherhood, personal development, sex, spirituality ... everything to stop me from just *feeling* the feelings I had stored in my body.

The day I let go of the rope of resistance was the day I finally let my body ***feel*** my repressed emotions

In feeling them and then letting them go I was able to create a path - from who I am to who I want to be.

The Path of Least Resistance.

With that path laid out, a clear flow of energy began to circulate - no blocks, no resistance - just a free flowing reality throughout my body.

Clear energy is powerful, much more powerful and lighter than the weight of stagnant energies. This is the very thing we are most afraid of,

The power we hold within ourselves.

"Our deepest fear is not that we are inadequate. Our deepest fear is that we are powerful beyond measure. It is our light, not our darkness that most frightens us." - Marianne Williamson

It is our very resistance to this *power* that is keeping us in a loop of misalignment - a dissonance that makes our journey through life seem harder than it actually is.

But all that is about to change - as you read this book, you will come to understand, where the resistance you hold originated, why it is there and most importantly how to recognise it *in the moment* - and then how to let it go forever.

In order to let go of the rope - we must recognise three key things

1. Who am I ?
2. What do I desire? (Aka the Golden Ticket Life)
3. What fears are holding me back?

In the pages that follow you will learn -how your conditioned state of "I am" came from your first interaction (or lack thereof) with masculine energy - in the form of man - your father, money and God

How your desires were shaped from your first interaction (or lack thereof) with the feminine - your mother, creativity and sexuality. How to find out what exactly your true desires are and how to tap into the power you hold that allows you to receive them.

And, you will learn, how the fears that are holding you back , are stories based on the main character role you created from your first interaction with the two energies we all hold within.

Those fears are nothing more than an energetic rope, that you have been holding onto all your life.

In a game of tug of war that you did not consciously sign up for

A tug of war you have the power to end at any point, by doing one simple thing....

Let go of the rope....

INTRODUCTION

Seville, Spain
July 2023

'It's been exactly 40 weeks since the day my life came crashing down around my ears.

40 weeks - the gestational period for the birth of new life

A version of me died, 40 weeks ago from today and it has taken nine long months to rebirth this new version who sits here this evening

I feel peace in my body unlike anything I have ever felt before.'

I had spent the first day there - wandering the streets of the beautiful, bustling city of Seville- my first time in southern Spain and it did not disappoint. I took in all the usual tourist hot spots, filled with humans from all over this planet enjoying the wonderful architecture and vibrant energy of a beautiful country steeped in tradition. I had a delicious lunch of ceviche - with a side plate of warm patatas bravas, I thought it would be rude not to. The two dishes did not exactly pair well - but I have never been too bothered about the conformity of pairing food - I much prefer a chaotic explosion of senses on my tongue. So the sharpness of the citrus soaked sea bass alongside the earthiness of the paprika coated potatoes suited my palate perfectly.<< Try saying that sentence out loud after a couple of glasses of wine... I dare ya.

The restaurant I ate in was extremely busy - the beautiful although slightly intimidating looking Spanish waitress gave me a great table right by the door, where I could look out into the square (it was far too hot to sit outside and anyway the tables were all taken) I complimented her on her outfit , a black gypsy style top worn with a tight fitting denim pencil skirt - and she flashed a grin at me, the intimidating look disappearing in an instant .. underneath all of our stories, women are very similar.

The feminine desires to be seen.

As I sat people watching and eating my lunch I became aware of a young, dark haired, woman standing next to my table , she was ever so slightly agitated - I could feel her nerves in my own tummy as I watched her fiddle with first her phone, then the silver bangle on her slender wrist. I heard her ask the same waitress (who it later turned out was actually the restaurant hostess - there to show everyone to their table but not actually serve the meals) in a strained voice, if she could order a drink while she waited on a table to become available

To which the hostess replied brusquely *No* - as she would not have a table number to ring the order through to

I watched this interaction with my usual childlike curiosity - my brain immediately wanted to know firstly, why the pretty young woman seemed so agitated and also if there was a way that she could have her drink without having a table number … surely there must be a solution to this..

'Excuse me' I said instinctively without pausing for thought - they both turned to look at me, inquisitively

You can sit here I have an extra seat - order your drink to this table

The hostess smiled at me even wider this time - glad to have a solution and get back to her place outside in the square ready to greet customers - hopefully customers who had pre-booked their table as there was definitely no space for walk-ins.

And so I ate my lunch whilst making small talk with my new companion for around twenty minutes or so, until a table became available for her

Amidst the conversation, I learned that she was from Germany originally, but had been living in Sydney, Australia for a decade. She was in Seville for three days at the wedding of a childhood friend - and had come via Faro in Southern Portugal - my home for much of last year. We spoke of places we both knew there and she relaxed more and more with each passing minute - in the midst of the chat my new friend (I never did find out her name, which is most unlike me) told me how she was terrified of flying. Really petrified. She poured her fears out onto the table we were sitting at - telling me how she would shake and tremble as the plane took off and how landing was even worse for her. She became more animated as she spoke of her anxiety at taking so many flights that week. As we spoke for a bit longer, it became clear her fear was not specifically of flying - but more of not being in control - she said she would be fine *flying* the plane herself … if only she had a pilots license (I think it is quite frowned upon to attempt to fly a plane with no license - certainly a commercial flight from Sydney to Dubai , it's around 14 hours long)

By the time this lady left my table I had learned a lot about this woman who just half an hour before, had been a complete stranger.

My friends laugh about this with me daily, how I meet so many people who offer me lots and lots of information about themselves in a very short space of time. As I sit here writing this tonight - I can count four other encounters like this - just this week.

There was the very handsome Nathan who organised my hire car at Glasgow airport the week before I arrived in Spain - a friendly Scot (just like myself) with the same open nature as most of my fellow countrymen - who, when he asked me if I had any questions (presumably about the hire car he was walking me across the car park to retrieve) I asked the first question that came into my head

Yes, I do - What is your favourite colour?

We both laughed and he told me it was black - then he proceeded to tell me that his sister had berated him for wearing black so often and so had taken him clothes shopping a few weeks earlier to buy new, brighter clothes.

By the time we got to the hire car - I had an insight into his new wardrobe and had discovered his sister was younger than him , by three years - but liked to look after him, which is often the way with sisters.

My friend Sarah got in the passenger seat beside me laughing and saying

Aly, I haven't spoken to one single person other than you, since I left home yesterday morning - how do you do this?

I am building an army … I said back to her with a grin and a shrug of my shoulders

On the flight back to London that same evening I sat next to Mick

Another total stranger , from Glasgow - flying to Oslo via London Stansted to watch an international football match that weekend

On our one hour flight to the capital, Mick told me all about his relationship with his father - how it shaped him as a young man and how it influenced the way he parented his lovely daughter Annabel - He very kindly, bought me a sparkling water … while being quite shocked that I turned down an alcoholic drink (there aren't many of us from that part of the world who don't drink alcohol) and spoke of his job as a prison officer and how it had affected his life over the past thirty plus years.

When we landed in London, Mick turned to me and said

'you are one of the easiest to talk to people I have ever met …

You should write a book '

I grinned at him and told him to look out for Least Resistance in a book store one day in the future … and I told him he would have a mention in it.

So Mick, on the flight from Glasgow to London Stansted - hello and I hope you remember me! Thank you for my sparkling water and the great chat.

Next there was the older lady I met on the way to Stansted the following day, when I was travelling back there to fly to Spain … she sat down across from me and opened the connection by asking me what time the train would arrive at the airport.

Ten minutes later she was telling me all about her trip from Cape Town the night before and how the airline had lost her luggage, much to her frustration. Within a few more minutes I knew about her family reunion coming up that week in Greece and what her favourite outfits were, that had been mislaid along with the suitcase.

Lastly - for this week at least - was Alex the Uber driver, we had a lovely 20 minute chat about the Universe, his son and the concept of Least Resistance - the premise of the book you are about to read…

Alex, if you are ever reading this - I hope you also read the two other book recommendations I gave you (Letting Go , David Hawkins and The Surrender Experiment by Michael Singer)

There are probably others I've connected with this week whose stories are lodged in my memory bank to come out at a later date.

I make friends everywhere I go, this is my unique soul gift - your gift is the the thing you do best with the least amount of effort

The thing I do best with the least amount of effort - is connect with people.

In person and in my writing.

Tim (remember the name, you will read more about him in the coming pages) remarked one time while watching me chat with a waitress in an Italian restaurant in the Maltese capital of Valetta,

' Ah you're actually interested in people … that's what it is … that's why this happens. You look people right in the eye and ask them how they are … for most people it's just lip service, but you actually care'

I was quite astounded at this statement… of course I care

These are my fellow humans.

Every single person on this planet.

We are all connected by an invisible thread - the thread of human existence.

Not only do I care about them - I love them

Every single person on this planet

I love them all. Including you reading this right now.

Tim would just laugh and shake his head at me when I spoke about love - and I speak about it a lot.

The concept of this book is about cultivating the art of least resistance - of bringing us back to our original innocent childlike nature of unconditional love and curiosity.

These two things - unconditional love and curiosity, are the foundation of our very happiness in life

If we can look at every single thing in our lives with a curious mind and learn to love everything that happens we will always be on the right path.

The path of least resistance.

The root of every problem we have in our lives is our resistance to reality - our resistance to what IS , along with our ego's way of attaching emotion to the reality going on around us.

Our ego is another word for the character we created in chidlhood.

We decide if something is good or bad, right or wrong, pleasant or unpleasant etc and then act accordingly.

When in reality - every thing just IS.

The attachment we give to what is, is subjective, based on our perception of it - and seeing as no two people on this planet have the same perception - none of these emotions are based in fact.

Perception is not fact. It is based on a story we tell ourselves and that story is centred around the emotions we feel.

So, if we can exchange whatever emotion arises in any given situation for a childlike curiosity and unconditional love for what is happening in the here and now, then we are practising *least resistance*

Here's an every day example

Alex - the Uber driver I mentioned above, was driving me to the airport to catch my flight - the train I was originally supposed to get to Stansted had been cancelled, it was rush hour - I was cutting it very, very fine with making my flight on time. So, an Uber was the quickest way to get from A to B. On entering the car, Alex asked me what time my flight was - when I told him, he whistled through his teeth - with a slight, almost imperceptible shake of his head…

No words needed - we were cutting it fine.

He knew it, I knew it, we all knew it.

I began to explain the concept of Least Resistance to him

' If I miss the flight it means I wasn't supposed to get on that plane - I will either catch a later flight or I'll go stay in a hotel and figure out what is going to happen next'

Alex looked at me in the rearview mirror - *'that's a good way to look at it'* was his reply

And I explained further, my fundamental belief - everything that happens to us is here to teach us something about ourselves.

'If I miss this flight perhaps the lesson I am supposed to learn is to give myself more time to get to the airport at rush hour, or maybe I was just supposed to meet you and we were supposed to have this chat … perhaps that's the lesson - but the main thing is that I apply least resistance

If I miss the flight my evening will be ***different*** *to how I first envisioned it to be - whether different means better or worse is determined by the story I attach to it - but different on its own does not have negative or positive connotations*

I can sit here and get upset about being late - which will not make you be able to get there any faster - but if I am annoyed here in this close

proximity, what I could do, is inferct you with that same angry energt, bringing your energy levels down to my level and that will permeate out into the world for the rest of the evening. My energy could then , have a knock on effect on lots of different people. Instead, I am not going to resist reality - maybe I won't make the flight - this is neither good nor bad … it just IS. Any annoyance or frustration is free to flow through me, but I will not hold on to it.

There are other flights - there will be another path - what ever is supposed to happen will be exactly what happens.

Least Resistance will just make it all easier and more enjoyable '

I exchanged the possible agitation at the situation for curiosity (what am I learning from this situation) and unconditional love - love for myself for not knowing what I didn't know I didn't know (that it would have been more beneficial to have given myself more time to get to the airport) and love for the situation - if I missed the flight I had learned a lesson for next time - this could only mean one thing - expansion.

Expansion is good.

Least resistance expands our consciousness. Every situations is an opportunity to learn.

Alex looked at me again in the rearview mirror..

'now you've got me thinking about something... my son, he dropped out of college to pursue a different career. I have been arguing with him about this for weeks ... maybe there is another way to look at this situation.'

I asked Alex how he felt about his son changing careers - *annoyed, frustrated ... agitated.* All cover up emotions for something else ... Fear . We got into a conversation about fear being the root cause of every perceived problem we think we have.

I gave him some homework (this is not the first time I have handed out homework to an Uber driver, im not gonna lie...)

When you get home tonight, grab some pen and paper and write down all the reasons why you are annoyed at this - keep writing until you get to the root fear.

The root resistance.

This is not about your son, his college course or the situation in front of you - this is about something in the past that is making you afraid, or an imaginary future that has not and maybe will not ever happen... write it down, you will figure it out. Find the fear.

Of course I made the flight on time … with a huge smile on my face and a new friend in Alex .

Another story - another lesson learned for Aly - do not try and get across London in rush hour traffic!

And uhm ... maybe stop giving Uber drivers homework...

Alex was upset with his son because of a story he was telling himself about the career change.

Humans have been telling stories since the dawn of time, we organise our thoughts in stories and then tell them to ourselves, using our inner voice as we go about our day.

First thing in the morning - *I will make some coffee, then do that thing, then I will xyz before doing abc. Oh I must remember to call my sister before lunch as she is going out this afternoon...*

the stories we tell ourselves dictate not only our daily lives, but *who* we are in the world.

My mother, was one of the greatest story tellers I have ever known, she could hold a room full of people in undivided attention with her anecdotes -

mostly centred around raising five young children, in the 1980's. With her Scottish wit and Irish heritage, Celtic storytelling had been weaved into her DNA for generations. Stories make an impact.

Human's have an innate desire to make an impact.

When I first began coaching women I was struck by how many of them were nearing burn out in their business due to the main story they were telling themselves

I want to make an impact on the world.

As though, all impact was some big thing *outside* of themselves, that they had to exhaust themselves in doing.We have been conditioned by modern society to believe that we can only make and impact by doing - when the biggest impact we can make is by being, most importantly being ourselves in the world.

I often tell my clients of my mother, a school dinner lady in a little Catholic school, in a small town on the west coast of Scotland - and the impact her stories made on those around her. On the day of her funeral in 2019, the church she was married in some forty odd years before, was packed out. Standing room only - everyone there to celebrate the life, and mourn the death of a wee quiet, somewhat nervous, dinner lady. I lost count of the amount of former school children who approached me that day, with a story about my mum - how she always remembered their favourite cake. How she offered a kind word if she saw someone upset, but most of all - they were able to recount a funny story she had told them at one point or another.

The stories my mother told, made an impact on the world, from a tiny corner that spread out all over this globe - I received similar messages from former St Gabriel's pupils far and wide. Flowers arrived from America, tears were shed in Australia - she made an impact, for sure. Her stories will live on in those people.

Stories impact everything we do.

Over the following pages, I am going to tell you a story - the tale of nine months of turmoil and the lessons I learned within that time.

The nine month period is not insignificant - it is the exact time frame for gestation of new life. I did not know it at the time , but when I looked back afterwards, I could very clearly see my story play out in three trimesters, much like the three stages of pregnancy.

I spent the first three months in a daze, unable to function properly at all.

The next three months I was able to create some kind of normality - albeit very different from any I had ever had before. I spent much of it in a foreign country, without my children.

And the final trimester, the final three months - I bloomed, I glowed, I followed a new path to a new life.

Then in the final week I gave birth to a new version of myself in Seville, July 2023 - ready to face my biggest challenge.

During those nine months I did not know that I was slap bang in the middle of a story - I was just going about my life, although in a state of distress for much of that time. The story came afterwards, as it usually does - when I was able to look back and *decide* how I would perceive what had happened in that time.

This is where I learned about the power of clear perception .

So, this is my story, of how i recognised the power I have to *choose* how I view those nine months.

it is a love story of sorts.

It contains heartbreak, revelations, new way ways of thinking and new ways of being. It is the story I tell myself now as I look back on what was a defining period of my life.

It was the middle passage for me - an epiphanous crossroads where I was forced to ask myself:

Do I stay the same?
Do I do as I have always done?

Or is this a chance to re-write the narrative, from here on in. With conscious awareness that I am the co-creator, the co-author of that story - using my energy and working with the guidance of the Universe, through the spiritual wisdom of the body to flow into the life of my dreams.

But this is not just my story, it is a *version* of the story of every single woman I have ever coached. It is a version of your story - or if you are man, reading this - it is a version of your wife's, your sisters or your mothers... or perhaps even a feminine version of your story too.

It is a tale as old as time - the spiral of life, the rise and fall.

It is heroes (heroines) journey, the descent and ascent we must all go through to learn the lessons of living.

My story has always been one of paradox. Full of love, but in the shadows of my subconscious mind, where I had repressed my emotions in childhood - it was also full of fear. That fear had built up a resistance that was prohibiting me from hearing the wisdom of my body. Along with the guidance of the natural flow of life it is there to help me create the path I was always destined to walk.

The root cause of resistance is fear

Fear that the reality we are facing is somehow going to harm us - fear is an emotion , emotion is energy in *motion.*

Things in motion are supposed to move - so if the energy is causing resistance this means it has become stuck somewhere.

Somewhere in our energetic bodies.

Energy is the most important commodity we have in this world - energy is everything.

It is the foundation of our very existence and we must protect it at all costs

From here on in, I want you to view your energy as liquid GOLD coursing through your being.

It is priceless, it is the be all and end of all of everything on this planet.

It is more important that your home, the amount of money you have in the bank, your parents, your kids, your dog, your favourite shoes, your granny, your job… you get my drift

Everything.

Why? Because our energy is constantly governing the world around us - this planet *turns* on the collective energy being emitted at all times - and every single human on this planet is a part of that collective.

If you wake up in the morning, after a restless night - with broken sleep and your energy is low as a result - pay attention to how you interact with the people around you, especially your kids.

What energy are they absorbing from you when you are feeling low energy - what are they learning about the world ?

Children are like little energetic sponges - they absorb EVERYTHING around them - put a group of kids together in a playground and watch as the excitement levels rise, they are all feeding off each others energy.

Our children are absorbing our energy more than they are listening to the words we say - which is why it is important that we not only pay attention to our own energy but also protect it at all costs.

So that the energy we give to *them* is clear and clean.

Now do you see why I said your energy is more important than your kids? Because it is your *energy* that literally shapes who they will become in the future. Children absorb energy in this way because they have not yet disassociated from their bodies in the way many adults have.

A few years ago a male client told me about an interaction he had had with his son just a few nights before. He was reading a book to the little boy just before bed, the story centred around a father and son bond, and so my client could see himself and his child in the characters. He told me how this caused him to become very emotional, he felt tears rise and a lump form in his throat .

He did not want his son to see him crying over a kids book (his words) so tried to swallow the tears back. His son, sitting on my clients knee, facing away from him - felt the change in energy and turned to look at his father. The little boy asked him if he was ok ... to which he replied *yes, yes I am fine*. Swallowing his emotions and continuing with the story.

When he relayed this to me on our call a few days later, he said his son had looked very confused. My client reflected afterwards on our call that he had taught his son to swallow his emotions too. I agreed and pointed out he had also taught him to question his own awareness of energy - by telling him everything was fine.

The little boy *felt* the energy change and was told by his father that this was not true. Children do not hear words, they feel energy - they feel it strongly in their bodies because they have not yet fully disassociated. We teach dissassociation to our children by telling them how to feel and how to act, rather than allowing their energy to flow and just acknowledging them for how they feel in that moment.

Today, after reading this - I want you to pay attention to the *energy* behind your words as you go about the rest of your day. If you are in a coffee shop, ordering coffee (or some kinda strange tea if that's your gig) - play with the energy of your voice and see how the barista reacts. Your energy influences your words, it influences how you hold yourself and how you connect with the whole world around you.

When speaking to your spouse or your child, think about the energy attached to the words you are using - then use your awareness to *influence* that energy to see what happens.

Energy speaks louder than words.

We cannot walk around with low level fear, agitation or anger in the root of our energetic bodies and expect it to have no an influence on the world around us.

When you are stuck in rush hour traffic, agitated to get to your destination - what energy are you sending out into the world

Anger, frustration, fear?

You are one cog in the great machine of this planet we call earth and you are sending out waves of anger, frustration and fear due to sitting in a queue of traffic

Due to a resistance of the current reality - and what is resistance ? A force that stops something moving or makes it move more slowly … so uhm yeah the traffic jam is your fault, you are causing those cars to move slowly with your energy... that's how powerful you are - you can slow a whole ass car down without lifting a finger

Just kidding , kinda...

Your energy matters , it is important - you are here for a very important reason - this planet, exactly as it is **right now** , is this way because *you* are in it - because your *energy* is making up part of the whole.

And this is true for all eight billion of us.

The collective energy of this planet, on which earth turns, is the way it is, because *your* energy is part of that collective. How cool is that?

You are kinda a big deal, here on earth - your energy is important to me - a complete stranger, because I know that it is playing an important role in the collective.

So if its important to me, it sure as hell better be important to you too.

Energy is not stationary - it is supposed to flow freely through our energetic bodies, specifically through our chakra system.

Side note here - I have not studied ancient texts, I do not know the ins and outs of the Vedas , I am just an ordinary Scottish woman from a very working class town - I was raised Catholic, we never spoke of energy in my family home in the 80's and 90's. My mother would not have known a chakra if it came up and shook hands with her in the street. The closest we got to India was a takeaway korma every now and then and even then we got the blandest of food for fear of stepping out into the unknown.

The system I created for my clients to clear their energetic blocks - and thus be able to walk the path of Least Resistance, literally came to me one day whilst I was meditating under a tree (more on that later) - I saw two triangles in my mind, one depicting the lower self and one depicting the higher self - when I rushed back to my hotel to write down what I had seen in my minds eye I realised the two triangles correlated almost perfectly with both the lower chakras and the upper chakras. From there, I began to use my system to teach my clients how to move stagnant energy around their bodies - and the results so far have been amazing.

Because what I have realised from coaching people, interacting with people and loving on people, is that not only is fear something we all carry inside of us - but that it is, more often than not, *repressed* fear , not present fear - that subconsciously runs the show in our daily lives.

Fear is the root cause of every problem we have - but fear rarely lives in the present moment.

So when we are in a fear filled state, we are, essentially, time travelling.

We are either judging our present reality based on a story from the past or we are afraid of an imaginary time in the future that may or may not arrive . And even then, if we are time travelling into the future it is almost always still from a story rooted in our past.

These stories created blocks in our energetic bodies - fears, swallowed in childhood that are now a build up of stagnant emotions

These blocks show up in our every day realities as problems - failed businesses, divorce, depression, physical illness, arguments with friends, traffic jams and many more

So if fear is the root cause of resistance, in order to understand the role it is playing in our lives we need to go back to the very beginning

To our own roots.

Because, in order to become who we are destined to be, we must first look at why we are, who we think we are.

PART 1

England, UK.
October 2022

"This is not going to feel good Aly"

I mean, friends, … he wasn't lying, I can tell ya.

I stared at the man I loved, as he delivered the words that followed that initial sentence, with a level of cool detachment I had only ever felt once before.

Six years earlier, in the February of 2016, I gave birth to my youngest daughter , Frances, at just 24 weeks gestation.

The three day labour, Frances' very traumatic delivery and the sixteen week hospital stay that followed, had been one of the most challenging times of my life.

But when I was rushed into theatre immediately following the birth of my tiny, 1lb 3 oz baby , I felt a sense of calm detachment flood my body.

I removed the oxygen mask to speak to the midwife who had accompanied me from the labour room and calmly asked her

Am I going to die?

She hesitated before replying, a look of panic crossing her face, before shaking her head - but it was too late, I had seen uncertainty in her eyes.

No, no Aly, you will be fine, just breathe

I felt a strange peaceful feeling flood my body as I accepted the reality of whatever would come next … even if that meant death.

And in that moment, I was certain it would mean death.

All at once, I felt complete acceptance of the reality of the present moment. It felt not of this earth, like I had somehow touched a level of being that had been out of reach before.

The nurse was correct, of course, and I did not die that day … would be slightly strange if I writing this from beyond the grave now, wouldn't it?

Really cool … but slightly strange also.

Taking the term ghost writer to a whole other level.

Frances and I both survived that day, she is now an eight year old bundle of fun and love - but I never forgot that feeling of total acceptance.

Six years later, I felt that same calm, detached acceptance, as I stared at Tim through my laptop screen.

It was one day after my 41st birthday, and life as I knew it, was about to come crashing down around my ears.

On that day, a seemingly ordinary Monday, the man I loved more than anything in the world, ended our relationship via an eight minute FaceTime call.

In doing so, he took away the masculine protection and provision I had finally found, after spending what had felt like, my whole life searching for it.

We ended the call and the feeling of acceptance vanished asquickly as it had arrived - in an instant I was transported back through my energetic body, to the unstable foundation of my childhood.

To the root of who I was conditioned to be.

Shame filled, grief stricken… terrified.

It was the straw that broke the camels back - the camel was me, my back was broken and I feared I would never get back on my feet again.

It would take nine long, wild months before I was able to view that phone call as the gift it truly was.

The gift of witnessing the trauma I held inside , as it rose from the subconscious of my body to the consciousness of my reality.

To then, be released, purged and alchemised into true power.

I spent most of those nine months running, running, running all over Europe, in a story that took me from London to Seville … via Loule, Edinburgh, Tangier, Lisbon, Faro, Zaragoza and Barcelona amongst other places.

I was running from the brutality of the painful emotions I felt inside - I was running from reality.

But with each passing month the realisation of what was really happening grew clearer and clearer. As I learned one important lesson after another - not least the realisation :

Our desires cannot flow to us if we are resisting the reality of all that we have in the moment.

And so, I stopped resisting reality - I slowed down more and more, until I came to a complete standstill in the Spanish city of Seville, July 2023… where I spent ten days sleeping late, eating delicious Andalusian food and exploring the sacred sites of what would soon become my favourite Spanish city.

And finally, when I stood still, completely still , present with my body, rooted in reality … I received another phone call … one that would show me how following the path of Least Resistance really is the easiest way to receive our true desires.

And I would learn of the magic held inside the bodies of women - the magic from the internal guidance system I had been ignoring since I was ten years old. I had to let go of everything I *thought* I knew in my mind, to learn the magical wisdom of my body.

That first phone call , the day after my 41st birthday, was the beginning of the death of who I was, it was a putting of an end to who I had been conditioned to be.But with that death, came the rebirth - the *conscious* creation of who I truly am

Who, deep down, I always knew I could be....

OUR ORIGINAL MASCULINE BLUEPRINT
MONEY, MAN AND GOD

Who Am I?

My first foray into the world of online coaching began as a behaviour change coach, specialising in weight loss, at the start of the Covid 19 pandemic in 2020.

Within six months of coaching women around their eating behaviours, I began to notice a distinct pattern with my clients - every woman in front of me had a story.

A story of how they had become the woman they were, and moreover, they viewed these stories as *facts* - cold hard facts, that could not be changed.

Every single story was formed in childhood, through the eyes of a child, looking at their whole world, standing in front of them in the form of two (or sometimes one) flawed human beings … their parents.

As I listened to these stories, I began to realise that my clients had unknowingly created their whole personalities based around continuous attempts to feel safe with their mother and father :

"I was the clever one, there was so much pressure on me to get good grades" said the straight A student - now terrified of letting her boss down, eating donuts on her break to numb the feeling of anxiety. She had joined my programme to lose twenty lbs - not realising that the fear of upsetting her father was the root cause of her sugar addiction. Every time she had a project to deliver to her male boss, her healthy eating went out the window.

"My older sister was always in trouble, I had to make sure not to upset my mother " said the people pleaser, a small business owner who gave too

much to her clients. Always exhausted … self medicating with wine every night after work, wondering why she was always tired and snappy with her kids.

"My father was always stressed - I was the only one who listened to his problems" said the serially single woman, desperate for love , pushing away every man who came too close - who had turned to food to comfort her in her loneliness

"Money was tight in our house, I've worked all my life to make sure my kids don't go without" an exhausted mother of three, working every hour God sends, disconnected from her husband, playing the role of mother and breadwinner - feeling constantly on the edge of failing at both.

She thought she was there to lose ten lbs so that she could feel sexier with her husband in the bedroom … no conscious knowledge that it was her resentment towards him that was causing the most problems. The subconscious projection of her own father onto her spouse, along with playing mother to him, was what had put out the spark in their relationship - not her love of potato chips.

"Women don't do that in our religion, we have to behave in a certain way" stifled, unseen, guilt ridden by her questioning of the culture she grew up in, knowing there is more out there but unsure of who she truly is without the heavy armour of her religious dogma.

Another woman, another story, subconsciously programming how she showed up in the world.

Every time I was faced with a story from a woman who felt unhappy with her life, unhappy in her current reality, I asked the same question:

> How old is the version of you who believes that story to be true?

The answers varied, from three years old to twenty three - one answer, from a male client in his thirties, when he mentioned a constant low level feeling of fear that was always in the pit of his stomach *"I think its always been there, since even before I was born, I think I probably absorbed it from my mother when I was in the womb"*

The fear he has carried since childhood dictating who he was in the world in adulthood.

The truth is , we cannot live peacefully in the reality of this moment if we do not know the roots of how we *perceive* that reality. And in order to know the roots of our perception we have to look at who we were conditioned to be in childhood. We have to learn how the child version of us saw the world.

We only live *here*, in the present, in the reality we have in front of us There is no other time other than this very moment that we are in now. But who we are in *this* moment is very much based on who we *were conditioned* to be. And that conditioning is based on our childhood, our parents, siblings, home town, ancestral trauma - a list as long as my arm. Thousands of fragments of every person we ever interacted with when we were deciding who we would be.

Recently I had a conversation with someone I know, a mother of three, frustrated with her life - lacking clear direction of what she wants for the year ahead and unsure of how to begin. Money worries have plagued her most of her adult life and now at almost forty she was growing tired of the constant cycle of not having enough.

I told her on the call - with every perceived problem, we begin in the present - then we look at how we came to this moment.

First question -

What do you need right now, in this very moment ?

She replied back almost instantly, *more money*

I had asked this question hundreds of times before (more often than not, the answer involves money) so I repeated my question with more detail:

listen to my question carefully, what do you need in this very moment, right now while you are sitting talking to me?

She looked at me in confusion, hesitating before replying, unsure if she was getting it wrong in some way:

Well, I would like more money, so that I can stop worrying about my bills, and do more things with my children.

I nodded.

Yes, I understand - but what do you need, right now in this very moment? I repeated slowly

I placed my emphasis on the words **need, right now** and **very moment**

I could see the frustration on her face, probably thinking why is this infuriating woman asking me the same bloody question three times

Eventually she understood what I was asking … and answered with a scowl on her face (her body telling me that she was not happy with the answer she was about to give)

Nothing

She was correct, in that moment she needed nothing - other than the breath she required to have the conversation with me.

In that present moment, she had everything she needed.

But her present was clouded, by what she believed she needed **right now.**

Now, this is not to say that she did not desire or indeed, even need more money to be able to do the things that she wanted to do - these things can also be true.

But there's a few important points here

What we *believe* we **need** and what we *desire* are often two different things. We have to treat them as such - say the two words out loud - need and desire. Feel the energy behind each word - one is rooted in fear one is rooted in love . Sure there are basics that we need - food, shelter etc - but most of us have them, we have everything we need. But we desire more - and this is ok, this is natural for all humans. What stops us from receiving our desires is the energy behind them.

The energy behind what we desire is rooted in who we think we are - and who we think we are, the personality we hold onto so tightly, is a false avatar we created as little kids .

So unless we become aware of who we were conditioned to be in childhood - what we desire, can and will be a struggle to receive or achieve.

For one simple reason - if what we desire is anyway based on fear,i.e we believe it is something we *need* to survive - it will likely never be fully enjoyed even if and when we attain it. As we will have a fear of losing it and thus losing the identity of survival we have attached to it.

Our identity and our desires go hand in hand.

So this comes back to the basic questions I ask repeatedly of all my clients:

Who are you ? What do you desire? What fears are holding you back?

Ok, so we had established the lovely lady in question needed nothing in that moment - but she *desired* more money to have what she would perceive as an easier life :

Less worry

More nice things with her kids.
But we know -

Our desires cannot flow to us if we are resisting the reality of all that we have in the moment.

Her current perceived reality was that she did not have *enough* money to do these things. This was causing fear somewhere in her energetic body. Repressed fear is a block - desires flow where there are no blocks. We had to find the fear and take action to eliminate it.

My next statement to her was not going to go down well, I could see it in her face, she looked pissed at me - so I pre-empted it with … *ok this might sting a little …*

"We are always getting what we need- so something about this current situation is desirable to you, comfortable - but also necessary for growth - what is it? "

She was not happy … just as I thought. I was glad there was a few hundred miles and a computer screen between us.

No-one wants to hear this - that there is something about their current situation that they require for growth - when the shit hits the fan, as it often does - we want to blame something *out there*, right?

Something outside of our control… well no, that's not *always* the case. And even if it *is* something that happens upon us that is outside of our control, we can always control our reaction to it.

We always have the power to choose how we see that which is happening around us. So perhaps, the situation has arisen simply to show us that power.

Upon further questioning we got to the root of the problem - my client did not know who she truly was, she did not know what she truly desired and until that conversation she did not realise that it was her own fears that were holding her back.

And most importantly - she did not know that those fears existed in her subconscious.

Who she *was* - was based on her upbringing, in a household with very little - where money was seen as something other people had, that was difficult to come by, that the earning of involved working your fingers to the bone. In her childhood, money was spent as soon as it was earned it was a resource that could run out - all of this was conditioned into her psyche without her conscious knowledge. She accepted a reality that money was difficult to hold onto based on a version of her that she had subconsciously created in the environment she grew up in.

What she desired - was based on money being the answer to all of her problems, more money would help her to feel safe, give her less things to worry about, it would offer her the protection and provision that she did not receive in childhood.

Her fears that were holding her back - money had emotions attached to it and the primary emotion was fear - *money is something that constantly runs out, it has an end point, I have to fight to get more, money is a struggle*

Her fears are a form of resistance - money is a form of energy, energy flows where there is no resistance.

The very reason she did not have "enough" money is because of the resistance that she had built up around it in childhood.

She was trying to get more money from a place of fear - true desire is based in love not fear, so she was creating a constant loop of chasing the thing she thought she needed most from a place of fearing she would never attain it and if she did get it she would just 'lose' it again. This was exhausting her.

Her ego - the personality she created in childhood, based on her first interaction with money was looping over and over the same wound cycle constantly -primarily her father wound.

The money problems she had based on who she had become would continually play out until she took *action* to break the cycle.

In order to take the action she first had to go back to the original blueprint of her own ego - the parts of her personality she had created to stay safe.

This began with her first interaction with the masculine. This blueprint was stored in her subconscious - the subconscious is the part of our psyche that contains every single experience we have ever had, good or bad.

Carl Jung referred to is as the shadow, the parts of ourselves that we cannot see but project onto others, in a kinda strange attempt to see it in the 'mirror' of the other.

"Until we make the unconscious, conscious it will rule our lives and we will call it fate". Carl Gustav Jung.

This truth by the great CJ, was none more so shown to me than when my relationship with Tim ended - the unknown emotions of my shadow, which had been following me through life, were brutally brought into my conscious mind by the ending of our relationship.

Every unspent emotion - fear, shame, guilt, anger, grief - all rose to the surface in the most ferocious manner - and they kept coming up, time and time again - until I let them rise, until I sat with them. Until I acknowledged them.

It was the final major setback in what had been challenging year. In the space of twelve months I had lost contact with most of my family, spent six months locked in a bitter court battle with my ex-husband and suffered two miscarriges in under three months - all while running my own business and mothering my two children. So the ending of our relationship caused me a level of fear that looking back , I can see was disproportionate to what was actually happening in reality. The disproportion was coming from the fears I had repressed when I was an actual child - I was looking at the world through the eyes of the ten year old child I had once been. She was running the show.

It was a horrible end to a horrible year - but if you leave this book with one truth, let it be this -

we learn more about ourselves and our true nature in the face of adversity than we ever will whilst at rest.

Of this I am 100% certain.

At the time I began writing this, I thought perhaps, I had had more adversity than others - for most of my life it certainly seemed that way to me. I spent the first four decades believing that life was happening *to* me, that I had no role other than to be the receiver of either good luck or bad. And there had been many times where I raged against an unknown entity at the bad luck I perceived to be on my path.

Until the day I realised that this entity lived within me - governed by the energy I vibrate at in any given moment.

Once seen it could never be unseen … (well, it can be ignored from time to time and it certainly is, I can tell you) - but it is always there in the background now as I go through life:

The knowledge that I am co-creating the experiences I am having, in real time.

That there is no enemy out there.

(Sidenote here - Nuance is needed when understanding this rather bold statement. Where there is an imbalance of power in any situation - i.e the sexual abuse I suffered in childhood at the hands of an adult, was something that happened *to* me. The enemy was out there - there was a clear imbalance of power there that I did not have any control over. Life is never black and white)

As an adult, however, I accept that I am the only person living in my Universe. The Universe that I view through the lens of my own self - and that 'self' is the version of me who creates the reality I live in.

My Univere literally does revolve around me .. just like yours revolves around you.

The way I create the narrative of my universe is through my energetic body - where my emotions are either stored or allowed to flow freely.

And the only person who has the sheer power to either store them or allow them to flow … is me

Emotions are literally energy *in motion* - so when we repress the energy that comes with the feeling (particularly the feelings we do not like to experience, such as fear, shame, grief and anger) they become stagnant and held in our energetic body.

Those stagnant emotions are the foundations of the stories we tell ourselves, that are governing how we view the world, how we react to the world around us and how we evolve in our journey through life.

Particularly how we evolve from conditioned states to enlightened states of being.

In order to understand where the conditioned states originated we must look into the very root who we believe we are.

Our original masculine blueprint.

Our first interaction with masculine energy in the form of money, man or God.

Masculine energy can be characterised by the following traits

Present

Protecting

Providing

Logical

Structured

Systemised

Grounded

Now, think of these traits in the form of the three most common symbols of masculine energy.

Man (firstly in the form of our fathers)
Money
God

in their highest forms they are all of the above, *all present, all protecting, all providing, all logical, all structured, all systemised, all grounded.*

Without protection - we feel fear. This is why our fears are rooted in the masculine.

Unfortunately, for most of us, we did not see all (or any) of these symbols of the masculine in their highest forms whilst growing up.

Any turbulence or trauma surrounding money, man or God was stored in the root of our energetic body in the form of repressed emotions.

And what is the most dominant repressed emotion?

You know it, you've heard me say it approximately 20,576 times already... Im probably gonna say it a few hundred more times before we get to the end of this story -

FEAR.

If your father was not present - either physically, emotionally or spiritually then there was no protection or provision in the household. This invoked fear.

If money was not present in the household there was no provision or protection. This invoked fear.

If God (in the form of any kind of spirituality or highest self energy) was not present there was no omnipresent provision or protection. This invoked fear.

Think about the little child version of you - or even think of your own children, what do they need most in the world?

Protection and provision

Protection from the lion at the mouth of the cave - figuratively or literally. When they are afraid they need to know they are protected from the thing that scares them.

They also need to be provided for.

Provision of shelter, food, love, nourishment, guidance, education

How we first viewed and interacted with the symbols of masculine energy, conditioned how we view the world.

Paradoxically - these symbols of the masculine may have been present in the physical sense, but traumatically so:

e.g an overbearing father who put pressure on you to conform. This invoked fear (of not being good enough)

Money was seen as a replacement to love - you were spoiled with material goods from a cold and distant father/mother. This invoked fear (of not being seen)

A God steeped in religious confusion who was portrayed as a wrathful being who punished sinners. This invoked fear and shame (friends, I could write a whole other book on the fears that this instilled in me)

All of these examples show us how the masculine may have been imbalanced in our childhood - this is not to blame our fathers, its important to understand that they were also conditioned in their childhoods by *their* fathers before them who were also conditioned by their fathers before them.

The list of trauma and conditioning goes back to the beginning of our family trees, of every family tree - we carry in our lineage, traits of people we have never met. Our ancestor's personality traits were handed down through the generations every bit as much as our hair colour and nose shape - and with that knowledge, we also know that we will pass our own traits (good and bad) down through future generations to descendants *we* will never meet. Not just to our own children but to their grandchildren's grandchildren.

Hugely powerful - we are the ancestors our great great grandchildren will one day speak of.

How *our* children view the world is first seen through the eyes of how they view their fathers, money and spirituality (their highest selves).

And with great power, comes great responsibility - so let's look at these three symbols of the masculine in our own past, and the responsibility these symbols had in creating who we are today :

Man

—

Take a few moments here to think about the masculine energy in your home as a child.

Was your father present? If yes, was he the protector of the home? If he was absent - who did the protector role fall to, perhaps your mother or an older sibling? How did they offer protection/provision to the family? Was your father's absence spoke of openly, or was it an silent absence that no one really acknowledged? How did your mother speak of your father?

Did you feel pressure from your him (or his replacement - i.e your mother) to behave in a certain way, did you conform or rebel to this pressure?

Think about the words your father used often - how he spoke to your mother, how he spoke of the world. How did other people treat him, what traits did he have conditioned in him from childhood, good or bad?

I once asked a coaching client to describe her father in five words, from the viewpoint of the child she was growing up … not from her current perception as an adult, the words she used were

Cold

Angry

Sad

Loving

Charismatic

These words are as varied as they are emotive - he was both cold and loving , charismatic and sad, paradoxical and yet intrinsically human. His inconsistent treatment of her - sometimes cold and distant, sometimes loving and nurturing created such confusion in her subconscious that she spent much of her adult life in relationships with men who gave her that same inconsistency. As this was the blueprint of her childhood , she thought it was normal, this was her normality. It was only when she became aware of this - by bringing her view of the masculine to the forefront of her mind, could she see the patterns she had formed from those perceptions. Then and only then, could she interrupt the patterns and create a new story.

Our fathers were the original blueprint for all men. How we saw our fathers in childhood shaped, subconsciously programmed how we would view all men throughout our lives. Until the day we become aware of this - then can we change it.

With this knowledge look at how you have viewed men in adulthood, do you want them to be a certain way based on the blueprint that you received?

What patterns do you have with men in your life, that have come from the subconscious conditioning of your father?
Patterns such as resentment, men never living up to your expectations, men 'letting you down' How were these patterns shaped by your first interactions with your father?

All of these questions will help you in becoming aware of who you believe you are in the here and now, based on your interaction with the very first man in your life.

Money

When we do not receive the protection and provision that we needed in childhood from our fathers we will replace it with another symbol of masculine energy.

Something that offers us protection and provision - money.

I have lost count of the amount of ladies I have coached over the years who replaced their husbands with money. They made money the King of their home. And why would we not? Women who were wounded in childhood by our fathers (so, that'll be all of us, to some extent or another) will be afraid to seek the level of safety they need, from any other man. They will instead, attempt to give themselves that safety from their own inner masculine. Women in 2024, are working like men - building wealth as a source of safety, protection and provision. In many instances this is great -

women feel empowered and safe. The problem it can create is, as women also carry the emotional load of the household - they are emotionally attached to the children in a way that fathers are not, this results in most women having two full time jobs - full time mother and full time employment. A lot of women I have coached, who rely on their own inner masculine to provide and protect them are disconnected from their husbands/partners. They have an underlying resentment towards them as they are not happy deep down that they are having to do the jobs of both sexes. This disconnection often shows up in the bedroom.

When money replaces the man of the house in the psyche of women, they associate their feeling of protection and provision the number of zeros in their bank account. They become their own protector and provider - and how this shows up in my clients is - those same women lose their sense of playful, flirtatious *feminine* mannerisms - the spark is lost in their marriage. They become rigid in their bodies and can no longer hear their internal navigation system - the wisdom of their intuition.

Energy is found within polarity - if a woman takes the role of the masculine by becoming the protector and provider, who is taking the role of the feminine?

Money and how we subconsciously view it was also indoctrinated into us in childhood.

What word/phrases did your parent use when talking about money , did they talk about the importance of savings? Did money have negative stories and connotations attached to it?

How your parents spoke about money and wealth will have a direct influence in how you view the energy of money, this is especially true for women.

Is the main masculine in your life today, man or money? Do you feel more protection from the amount in your bank account than you do from your husband or partner? Who makes the main money decisions in your household? Are you happy with the current dynamic?

The problem we have if we anchor ourselves to this masculine energy in the form of money, is, there is always a risk that it can be taken away. Money is outside of ourselves, it lives in the world of matter - the true, highest form of masculine energy lives *within us* and can never be taken. Which is why the most important symbol is the one that can never leave, never be taken from us - is the most revered symbol of the masculine, of all time. ...

God

The highest form of Masculine energy - the God within us all.

"If I could wave a magic wand and give you something, just for today, something you would like right now, what would it be?"

My sister, younger than me by four years, well used to my somewhat strange questions, stared back at me through the phone.

We had been on a FaceTime call for around an hour and the chat had swung from teenage crushes (hers, on a random butcher in our hometown) to the death of our mother and the whereabouts of her ashes. My sister currently had the urn in her home. On top of her wardrobe to be precise, much to my amusement … I pointed out that this was in great view of her bed… where she and her partner have sex. Laughing I told her Mary is always "watching over her" ….My sister was not best pleased with my joke.

She had announced whilst discussing our mothers remains , that she no longer believed in any God - that when we die "the lights just go out" that's it , game over.

I told my sister my belief, that there is no God outside of us, God is merely a symbol of Divine masculine energy in its highest form, and we all carry a fragment of that energy within us.

So in essence - we are all God.

She looked at me like I was crazy… we were raised Catholic, this would have been blasphemy in the eyes of our mother. The Catholic version of God we grew up with, lived in the sky and was always watching over us to make sure we did not commit sins

Sins such as - missing Sunday Mass, not doing penance during Lent and not confessing all of our sins as a seven year old child to a man behind a curtain …

He did forgive all sinners though for committing the sins in the first place… confusing.

I went onto explain further to my sister -

God is the highest symbol of masculine energy on earth

The highest masculine - the most protecting, the most providing, the most grounded

All the traits of the masculine in its highest, most divine form.

And what is even more amazing is we can commune with God at any given moment, simply by talking to the highest masculine version of ourselves. No need to sit on a cold bench in St Andy's chapel every Sunday.

God performs miracles, He can make anything happen ... that is what he had been taught in St Andrew's way back in the 80's - so if God can make anything happen.. we can too. We can perform miracles.

Caroline just wasn't having it - so I tried to explain my theory in real terms:

"If I could wave a magic wand and give you something, just for today, something you would like right now, what would it be?"

She laughed a bit scornfully and said *someone to come and tidy my house for me* my next question - *do you believe that you can have this thing that you want?*

No - and then she paused… *well my friend Laura would help, if I asked. But I wouldn't ask, she is busy*

I am 100% certain Laura would help my sister tidy her house - I do not know a single woman, walking this earth, who when asked for help from a friend, would not do everything in her power to make that happen… especially as women rarely ask for help.

I relayed this to my sister who nodded vehemently, agreeing with me - of course Laura would help. Most woman would. My sister could stop a random woman in the street outside her house to ask her for her help and I would bet a lot of money the answer would be yes.

So I pointed out to her - you can have anything you want in life , you can make anything happen… but you have to take the *action* to get it . She was not best pleased about this - she wanted the help, without having to do the thing that would get the help. But she did laugh and agree - she could have what she wanted - she just wasn't willing to ask Laura.

I see this a lot in the online coaching industry - women being told that they can manifest anything - money, their dream job, the man of their dreams - all by sitting on their ass and waiting for it to show up.

This is a misinterpretation of what manifestation actually is.

Yes, you can receive all of the above - but you must be in alignment to receive it - and that alignment usually involves taking aligned action.

Think of our desires, anything you want right now, as the divine child created by the energy of the masculine and feminine working together.

The feminine desires, the masculine makes manifest in the world of matter

this is true for all - both men and women.

but especially true for the energies we hold within ourselves - it is our *inner* masculine that first provides for us. The highest, most clear version of this inner masculine is God - and just like I said :

There is no enemy *out there* -

There is no God *out there*

We hold the energy of God *within* us.

We are God.

In order to commune with our inner masculine - God, we have to make sure our bodies are not in a state of fear. When we are in a state of fear we are working from ego - the version of us we created to keep us safe. The ego lives in the mind and constantly tells us stories to stay small and forget our power. To convenve with God, our inner masculine we must use the body.

We must come out of our heads and back into our bodies.

The two main ways I ask my female clients to do this are

1. Sit with both feet on the ground, close your eyes, place your right hand over your heart or your womb space. Take three deep breaths - slowly, in through your nose, out through your mouth

Centre yourself, breathing deeply - then asked your inner masculine a very simple question

This could be -

what is the next step on my path?

Should I do x or should I do y ?

What do I need right now in this moment in order to move forward?

These questions should be as simple as possible. The answer will flood your body** - trust the first answer and then take action on it.
(**Caveat, here, a lot of my clients, when I ask them to do this in the beginning, tell me they cannot hear anything. They cannot hear their innver voice. This is for a whole host of reasons many of which I cover in my online programme, The Way of the Women, but this is also a practise and

may not be achieved the first time you try it. Like any form of practise we must try it over and over again to get better at it.)

If the question is - what should I do in this moment and the answer you hear is rest

Then REST. God has spoken. Your inner God.

The second, very effective way to hear your inner masculine is to repeat the steps above but instead of sitting with both feet on the ground you can do so from the bath.

That's right, regular homework for all my coaching clients is this - run yourself a long, warm, luxurious bath and ask the God inside of you what the answers are to the burning questions within. Trust the answer that comes and if needed, take action on that answer.
Whether you sit on a chair with your feet on the ground or lie in a nice warm bath, the foundation of what you are doing in this moment is the same.

You are being still.

The paradox of *creating* our new reality is this, we cannot move forward without first sitting still.

I see many clients who believe they are moving forward in life, and I can see why - they are constantly moving, constantly doing - but what they often fail to see, is that they are running on a hamsters wheel. They are creating a lot of movement but not actually getting the desired outcome.

And I should know - I had been running on that same hamsters wheel all my life - that phone call from Tim in October 2022 was my inner God finally raising his voice so that I could hear him over the running.

My inner God sent my outer God (Tim) to deliver the words I had been ignoring -

He literally told me - *This isn't going to feel good Aly …*

And he was right - but something had to change so that I could *feel* anything.

Entering therapy in 2020 was the initiaion I needed to understand the distortion of my original blueprint at a cognitive level. I spent months *talking* about my feelings. And honestly - it changed my life, finally being able to say the words I needed to say out loud

But the break up with Tim, was the initiation I needed to *feel* all those feelings at a body level.

I had to *feel* the fear of abandonment - that I orignally felt and repressed

I had to *feel* the grief that I originally felt and repressed

But most of all I had to *feel t*he anger ...

PART 2

November, 2022
Loule, Portugal

Three weeks after Tim and I separated I found a small, hard, pea shaped lump on my right breast one Saturday evening, just after I had put my youngest child to bed. I was in the Algarve with Frances, then aged six , who had just gone to sleep after a long fun filled day at the beach. We were both exhausted. I sat down on the sofa tired, dazed and still confused as to why my life had been thrown into such disarray. I opened my laptop and began writing, journalling my thoughts and feelings from the day. I had been doing this every evening since early October. Suddenly, my right hand, seemingly of its own accord, left the keyboard and slowly but decisively touched my breast , exactly on the spot where the small lump had formed.

At this point I had been running on adrenaline for three weeks, barely sleeping, eating next to nothing each day, while trying desperately to maintain a semblance of normality for my children. I was still in a state of shock at the sudden ending of my relationship and the subsequent refusal of Tim to even speak to me. Most of my belongings were still in our apartment - but Tim was avoiding my texts.

We had gone from speaking daily for two years to barely exchanging a dozen words, overnight, I felt a level of abandonment and confusion unlike anything I have ever known. This had come less than a year after I had plucked up the courage to tell my family of the sexual abuse I suffered in childhood. Their traumatised reaction was one of blame and anger towards me - and literally overnight I lost all contact with 99% of my family.

Tim and my daughters were the only family I had at this point and now the head of our family was gone. Taking with him the leadership and protection he had provided for us all while we were together. Unlike every other time I had experienced struggle in my life, when I had just dusted myself off and got on with it, this time felt different.

This time, I could not seem to pick myself up off the floor.

I smiled throughout the day for Frances, deflecting her questions asking where Tim was by telling her he was busy working until I felt strong enough to break the news to her. I told Eilidh (my first born, then aged 22) over and over again that I was doing ok, *Ive been through worse, its just a breakup - I will get over it,* … but the reality was, I was struggling more than I ever had in my life. It was like a damn had burst somewhere inside of me and everything was rushing through my psyche at lightning speed.

All the while, there was a version of me, standing at the side watching myself pretending I was ok, knowing I really wasn't. I felt like I was floating through earth - everyone else looked the same, acted the same, spoke the same, but I was different.

I was falling apart.

So, when I found the lump that evening, if I am being completely honest - there was a split second flash of relief … *maybe this is cancer, and I will die - that will make it easier for them (my daughters) if I just leave this way.* I was shocked to my core when I heard those words coming from an exhausted, heartbroken version of me, where did those thoughts come from? I did not want to die. Was I really so exhausted with life that this seemed like the best way out?

I sat there in the dark touching the lump, asking myself … is this serious, is this cancer? The answer I heard was no - nothing serious. Just a physical reminder of what repressed trauma can do in our bodies. I believed my inner voice but I also knew I would have the lump checked out by a doctor, to be on the safe side. The lump was telling me something - I had to find out what that something was. My body was speaking to me, it was up to me to listen.

I took Frances back to her father in the UK on the 31st of October and returned the very same day, to the Algarve. Tim and I had rented a beautiful apartment five minutes from the beach, where I had spent 50% of my time while Frances was with her dad. I considered Portugal to be my home as much as the UK - my time had been split almost equally between the two for most of 2022. Tim had emailed to say he was out of the country for a few weeks so I was able to go and collect my belongings from our home. I sat in the apartment still in shock that we would no longer be living there together - looking around at all the beautiful furniture we had spent months picking out. Reliving memories of me dancing in the kitchen whilst cooking, Tim lying on the sofa in our open plan front room watching me in amusement. I thought about the day we moved in, how Tim had stood behind me with his arms around my waist, as we put the key in the lock together - so full of excitement for the memories we would make in our new home.

I sat on my beautiful new sofa and let the tears fall, releasing the sadness - before leaving my key on the kitchen counter and closing the door the door behind me.

The next day I booked an appointment in a private hospital in cute little town called Loule - just a few miles from our apartment. I checked into an air bnb within walking distance of the hospital and tried my best to not worry about the upcoming tests.

I had a mammogram within a few days and was told I could return to collect my results in person, ten days later.

My maternal grandparents had both died relatively young, of cancer in the 90's and early 2000's - and in 2019, my mother had died suddenly and tragically of sepsis, aged just sixty three years old. In the weeks that followed finding the lump I had thought about my mother daily. How her death had affected me and my siblings and how it felt to be a woman without her mother in the world. I did not want that for my daughters.

I did not realise how afraid I was of death, until I walked into the hospital ten days later to receive the results of the mammogram.

My legs felt like jelly as I approached the reception desk in the outpatients clinic and asked if my results were ready. The lady behind the counter smiled kindly as she handed me a brown envelope. With shaking hands I pulled out the white paper on which the results were printed… entirely in Portuguese. A language I sadly, had not learned enough to understand at this point. I looked up quickly, panic rising in my throat, as I asked the receptionist if she could translate it for me- she shook her head and told me in broken English that she was not permitted to do so. She pointed to the very long line of people waiting to see the doctor and said I could join the queue.

I did not know what to do - so I turned and walked away without saying another word.

I stumbled out of the hospital into the sunny streets of Loule , wildly searching for someone to help me - in my panic filled state it did not even cross my mind to use the internet to translate the results. Something that made me smile a few hours later when I realised that would have been the obvious solution. I literally had a translator in my hand. Fear not only freezes us physically - it freezes our ability to think straight.

Across the street was the small cafe I had been working from most mornings that week - the waiting staff there had begun smiling in recognition when I walked in each morning with my laptop. Perhaps someone could help me there - I walked into the cafe and straight to the counter where an older lady I had noticed for the first time, the day before, was standing . She had an air of ownership around her and I had assumed (it turned out, correctly) the cafe belonged to her. I thrust the envelope towards her asking

Can you translate this into English please

She studied the papers, brow furrowed, rubbing her chin and glancing up at me every few seconds

Just say the words

Just say the words

Just say the words

I thought

I repeated the dreaded word over and over in my head

Cancer, cancer , cancer

I searched her face for clues as a few of the young waitresses gathered around her. All in their 20's, Portuguese, open and friendly. They had each brought me my coffee at one point or another in the course of that week - now they looked at me curiously. I searched their eyes for signs of pity.

The older lady spoke to them in rapid Portuguese still not saying anything directly to me - I thought my eyes would bore holes in her head by this point …

When suddenly she looked up and said two words in English - *follow me*

I followed her through the cafe - past the counter into the back of the cafe , past a few confused looking kitchen porters, past the rows upon rows of lunches ready to be served

To a rotund, older gentleman wearing a chefs hat with a dishcloth slung over his shoulder.

The chefiest looking chef I had ever seen.

The lady spoke quickly to him as she handed over my letter - while I looked at him with pleading eyes

Please just make it quick

My eyes told him, *please just get this over and done with*

He scanned the letter quickly and almost immediately placed his hand on my shoulder

Not cancer

were the first words out of his mouth

not cancer he repeated, smiling, nodding at me

I thought my legs would give way from under me

He reached out and hugged both me and the older lady together as I repeated *obrigada, obrigada* over and over with tears streaming down my face. I just allowed myself to be hugged by these two precious strangers. I really needed it.

The chef went onto explain that the lump I found was a cyst, I needed a follow up appointment to have it drained or removed if necessary, but *definitely not cancer* - he repeated kindly for good measure.

As I walked back through the cafe the waitresses formed a little line smiling and clapping their hands, some of them rubbing me on the back as I passed them by.

The kindness and love of these strangers, in what was surely one of the scariest days of my entire life will never leave me. People are beautiful, we want to connect with each other, we want to share good energy. Those people in the cafe, their love lifted me up as I walked out into the sunshine.

I sat outside the cafe on a bench and put my hand on my womb asking myself what all of this meant.

Why was I there, miles from home, alone with all of this happening

What was the message my body wanted me to know

I heard two words

Stay still.

The very thing I had refused to do since that horrible phone call in early October.

The very thing I had refused to do for most of my life…

Stay Still.

Did I have what it took to stay still … to sit with my emotions?

I wasn't filled with confidence but I had heard the message loud and clear. The decision to whether or not I followed the wisdom of my body was entirely up to me....

OUR ORIGINAL FEMININE BLUEPRINT MOTHER, SEXUALITY & CREATIVITY.

What do I desire?

For as long as I can remember I was angry at my mother.

All through my teenage years, my 20's and most of my 30's

It was just this thing, it was always *there* in the background, a low level resentment, an irritation that gnawed at me whenever I interacted with her. Of course I loved her, I spoke with her often, I visted her when I could. But there was always something underlying, between us, that I could never put my finger on.

She died, suddenly, in 2019 - she was just sixty three years old - here one day, gone the next.

And then - I was angry at her for dying.

I stood over her coffin in the funeral home a week after her death, looking down at the body that had once housed my mothers consciousness. Now just an empty shell - she was gone forever and just as I had always done, I repressed my feelings.

It was the only thing I knew how to do.

Around two weeks after the funeral I needed a stronger numbing method to distract me from my anger - not knowingly of course, I just went out one day and bought a bottle of wine without really thinking about it.

I had one glass on the first night

Then two glasses a few nights later

Within a month or so I was drinking a bottle of wine most evenings , within two months that was looking more and more like two bottles. I had always had trouble sleeping at the best of times and so I could tell myself that the wine was helping me sleep.

This was a good thing... right?

The ego is very clever - it can convince us of almost anything.

I had no idea I was using the wine to repress my anger.

Much like I had no idea I had used over-working constantly all my life to repress my shame

Just like I had no idea I had used motherhood to distract me from my fears from the age of 18 years old.

That's the thing about the methods we use to numb ourselves from the truth - they generally do a very good job at what they are supposed to do… making us forget how we really feel.

For a period of around eleven months I drank nearly every single night. The knowledge that I could pour myself a glass of wine at some point late afternoon was the thing that got me through each day. That along with working more hours than I had ever worked before and trying to be super mum to my children at the same time. Oh and baking cupcakes - for reasons unknown, I also baked a ridiculous amount of cupcakes in that time.

I gained weight (probably due in part, to the cupcakes) , I became more and more irritable … I descended further and further down a spiral of despair. Respite from that despair only came in a ten day holiday to visit my childhood best friend , now living in Chicago. Frances and I spent ten days being looked after in the home of someone who had been like a sister to me for most of my life. Denise took the place of my mother in those ten days, she cooked my meals (when we were not eating out and we ate out a lot!) She brought me coffee in the morning, wine in the evening - we laughed, reminisced and generally acted like two teenage girls again. It was the first time I had laughed in months, maybe even years.

When I returned from Denise's, around six weeks before Christmas 2019, I became ill with a strange cough that lasted into 2020. I visited the doctors office and the local hospital emergency room two or three times in the space of two months. No one could find anything wrong with me other than a "100 day cough" that could potentially last, well, one hundred days apparently. There was nothing I could do in the meantime other than wait it out. I woke that Christmas 2019, filled with sorrow and dread, the very first Christmas morning I had ever experienced, without a phone call from my mum asking if "Santa has been yet". My life had changed forever. I spent the day in my kitchen, mostly alone, listening to my mum's favourite songs whilst crying and burning Christmas dinner. Eventually going to bed, very early in the evening, at the same time as Frances, desperate to get the day over and done with.

The last week of 2019 passed in a daze.

2020 began uneventfully - I had no idea what was in store for me - or that it would be such a pivotal year in my life.

I still do not know why I poured the last glass of wine down the sink one Saturday afternoon in early 2020, just two weeks shy of the first anniversary of my mother's death.

To this day, I have no inkling as to why I decided *that* was the day, when enough was enough

But I did.

When I look back, I think perhaps its was the hand of God, something inside of me just clicked. Something not of this world, told me from somewhere deep inside - *its time to wake up from this fog Aly.*

Within six weeks of giving up alcohol I entered into psychotherapy for the first time and I was finally able to say, out loud, the words that had haunted me for most of my life,

I am angry at my mother.

I grew up in a very tribal community, in the west coast of Scotland, the landscapes may be different but the clan culture of our ancestors was ingrained in us all deeply throughout childhood - this is a place where blood is thicker than water, and no matter what happened inside the tribe - you do not question the leadership.

That leadership came in the form of our parents.

The day I said out loud to my therapist that I was angry at my mother was one of the hardest days of my life - I felt like I was going to die.

In fact a version of me did die that day

The people pleasing, just get on with it, stoic version of myself that I inherited from the very woman I was angry at.

I dropped all sense of stoicism I had absorbed from her and just let myself see the anger that had been there all along. I opened my mouth and let out every unpleasant thought I had ever had about her - pure vitriol burst forth from somewhere deep inside me.

But I realised something when I voiced all the reasons why I was angry at her - my mother was always afraid , her body was wracked with fear since I could not remember when. Every reason I gave for my anger at her, seemed to stem from her fears - I did not see it until I spoke it out loud.

I know now, the *real* reason why I was angry at her - it was because I was afraid too - it was my fight or flight kicking in in direct response to her fear, and I had chosen fight… in the form of anger.I matched her energy - but chose the opposite fear response.

My mother did not choose anger as a way to cover up her fears - she chose people pleasing instead and I was angry at her for that most of all.

She had her own numbing techniques of course, that I had silently judged my whole life … you see, I thought I was better than her because my numbing methods were more socially acceptable - in my eyes at least.

She smoked heavily - I would never smoke, I said over and over …oh, but I gossiped and judged. Every bit as toxic.

She drank vodka - I was way more classy… right, because I drank expensive wine. The irony is not lost on me these days.

She never stood up for herself - me? I fought with everyone and anyone. I argued incessantly with everyone who dared to cross my path - from taxi drivers to strangers online.

My mums go-to fear response was freeze and fawn - mines was fight or flight (most often fight) we were cut from the same cloth, I just could not see it.

But the day I was able to say I was angry at my mother was the day I realised we were more alike than different.

It was the day I was finally able to see her for what she truly was.

Just a woman - trying to live in this world, trying to do her best with what she had. Trying to do anything she could to quell the fear she had buried inside.

We were the same, but now the time had come for me to acknowledge all the fears I had buried, something my mother's generation did not have the resources to do.

I did not just enter into therapy for myself, I entered into it for my mother and all the women who came before her in my family tree.

The stoic, distraction filled numbing techniques would stop with me - I would not pass them down to my own two daughters - I was determined to make sure of that.

To get to the love, the joy and desire for life - I first had to recognise everything that was in its way

Anger

Shame

Fear

I had to become *aware* of the anger first

The death of my mother, and the therapy that followed- was the first initiaion into consciosuness of how I viewed her, my first interaction with the feminine. The first woman I would look into the 'mirror' of - it would be some two years more before I was able to turn that lens inwards, to feel all the emotions I *felt* about myself.

Having ill feelings towards the woman who gave us life is one of the greatest taboos in our society. I have coached hundreds of men and women who have sat across from me and told me heartbreaking stories about their childhoods - that almost always end with

but she is my mum, I love her, she was trying her best

You are probably thinking this too - as memories come to mind of times when you have been angry at your own mum - *she was trying her best*....true, very true - she likely was trying her best, my mother certainly was.

But I learned that I could love her and be angry at her at the same time. I just had to acknowledge the anger.

Ive asked my clients countless times -

How old is the version of you who is angry at your mum?

12 years old - when she wouldn't let me stay out late with my friends

15 years old - she was always complaining about my dad

8 years old - she was always working ... she never listened.

A few years ago during an in-person coaching day with a male client , I began taking him through a guided meditation to find his anger. This very successful businessman, married with kids - had been telling me for weeks that he was growing more and more agitated in his work life and could not get to the root of why. We had been delving into his childhood, where he said honestly that he had always been a little 'frustrated' at his mother growing up, but understood why she behaved the way she did.

Lying on the floor of my office, in silence, breathing deeply, I asked him to imagine his mum was standing in front of him, looking the way she did when he was a child - I asked him to tell his mum what he wanted to say to her as a ten year old boy. He opened his mouth to speak:

'you are fucking idiot - why do you always believe him over me, I fucking hate you'

the 'him' he spoke of was his younger brother - a seemingly insignificant sibling rivalry that had long been forgotten - but the repressed anger of that ten year old was the tapping on his shoulder that had followed him around since childhood. It was the anger that showed up in his business, his relationships, his fathering of his children - stemming, in part, from a fear of being overlooked in favour of his brother, of being compared and not being good enough.

As a child all he wanted was to be seen by his mother - as an individual, not in comparison to his sibling. That desire to be seen and the fear of not measuring up had been lurking in the shadows of his subconscious for most of his life. It affected a lot of his day to day interactions with the world - an underlying fear that he was not good enough. He had to recognise the original anger, a cover up for fear - to be able to recognise it again in present day. He had to feel the anger that he had repressed in order to feel it again in the present and then let it go.

This was life changing for him. It's been life changing for me, recognising my anger - my fear, around my mother enabled me to understand my true desires in life.

If the root of who we are , stemming from our first interaction with our fathers, is the house of:

Who Am I ?

Then, our first contact with our mother - our original feminine blueprint - is the house of:

What do I desire?

But, if we are so filled with fear and anger that we do not believe our desires as within our reach, how do we create?

The truth is, people can and do create from a body filled with fear, but our creations will forever be marred in instability. Built on a bedrock of agitation - and we will never be able to fully enjoy what we have created in the moment.

Around the time I first attended therapy, I was being mentored by my very first business coach - Tim (yes, the one who some two years later, broke my heart, t*hat* Tim. Also the man who first coached me in making money and in doing so, inadvertently, set me on the journey to healing my father wound)

On our very first mentoring call Tim asked me a very specific question

"*What is the big dream, Aly ... what does your dream life look like?*"

I was blown away by this question - I felt my body literally jerk in shock - I must've sat there for half a minute gawping like a goldfish.

Bus as soon as I opened my mouth to speak, a stream of consciousness came, seemingly out of nowhere

" *I want to take all of this shit off my face"*, I said as I pointed to my face full of heavy make up that I had worn daily since I was a teenager. "*I want the world to see the real me,I want to stop working so many hours! Oh and I want a big house in the sunshine, where I can be barefoot in my garden, baking my own bread*"

I was as surprised as he was by the velocity of my words - the energy behind them. I had no idea where they came from - but they felt good. They felt *real*

But when I left that call with Tim that day, guess what I felt?

Anger.

There she was again - anger, my go to emotion.

And now that anger was directed at Tim - for asking me about my dream life.

How very dare he!

No one had ever asked me that question before - I had no idea that there was a dream life out there, nor that I could live it.

I very quickly realised, I was not angry at Tim, of course, I was angry at myself - because my life at that time, was very, very far from the dream life I had blurted out on that call.

Anger is an awesome emotion - it is an emotion that moves us - no one really wants to stay still with rage, we want to stand up, move about, maybe throw things, maybe punch something
(something, not someone)

Anger forces us to do something - *only,* and I cannot stress this enough, *only* if we do not repress it.

Every single client who has sat across from me in the past few years, regardless of whether they were male or female, has had an issue with anger, and by issue, I mean they have repressed their anger in the past and it has come back to bite them on the ass at a later date.

Recognising anger, moving anger and ultimately *letting go* of anger (which admittedly I did not learn to do properly for two more years) is a game changer.

I used that anger I had after that initial call with Tim, to propel me forward towards my dream life. I took all the makeup off my face and I started to show the world the real me.

I told the truth - I told people how I really felt for the first time in my life. And it came as no surprise, to see it scared a lot of them away.

One of the first things I did with my new found courage for truth, was to finally tell my family about the sexual abuse I suffered in childhood. I was devastated by the repercussions of that conversation (and so were they) but something kept me going throughout the months that followed - I had told the truth. I had shown them the real me.

I stopped people pleasing - I began to tell people how I really felt - and the authenticity was not always accepted. But I persevered with it knowing I was on the right path.

My mother had lived her whole life people pleasing out of fear. When I stood over her coffin that day in 2019 I made a promise to her, that I would not do the same. That I would not leave my two daughters with the legacy she had unknowingly passed onto me.

It took 12 months of numbing the fear with alcohol and seven months in therapy before I was able to stand up and tell my devastating truth to my family, but in doing so I was able to see a clearer path forward than I ever had before.

Only after I had looked at my anger, my fear, and my shame - could I truly look at my desires.

Only then, could I stand up and say with all certainty

This is what I desire - this is what I want my dream life to look like.

The house of my mother - when cleared of the repressed emotions I inherited from her, was filled with pure raw, clear sexual energy.

Ready to create the life of my dreams - the Golden Ticket Life.

The day after Tim asked me on that initial call, what my dream life looked like, I was sitting on the beach near my home in the UK - looking out into the water, thinking about my answer to his question.

The big house, the garden - where did all of that come from?

What did i dream about when I was a little girl? What was my dream job as a child? I had repressed so many of the traumatic memories that I could not remember the innocent ones. I sat there trying to remember my childhood dreams when a clear memory flashed into my mind.

I think it was from my teenage years although with the passage of time I cannot be certain, but I do remember this was a recurrent dream. I mean an *actual* dream, at night in the land of nod. I would, intermittently - I think over the course of some years, dream of a house that I had never been to in 'real life' . When I closed my eyes that day on the beach, I could see the house in my minds eye, clear as day , in a lot of detail. It was a beautiful white house, with a big blue front door, windows with blue ledges and a garden that stretched as far as the eye could see. There were flowers, purple and pink, lining the path to the front door. The house was on a hill, surrounded by lots of green grass, trees, secluded - with a beautiful sea view in the distance.

It was my dream house ... literally.

I thought about the life that would afford a house like that, the person I would have to become to live there - I had struggled financially my whole life - my parents had struggled financially and their parents before them (althought slightly better off) were the same.

What kind of person lived in a house like the one I had dreamt of - someone who was fiancially stable, who respected money, who used their talents to build wealth - who could afford a house with a direct sea view.

I turned from where I was sitting on the beach and looked behind me -there sat a row of perfect houses overlooking the sea. I knew from looking in the windows of the estate agents on the main street near my house, that these properties cost well over a million pounds. *I want to live on that street*, I thought as I sat there.

At the time, I lived three streets back from these houses, in a little terraced cottage, it was a nice enough house.

No sea view, big blue door or flowers in the garden.

It was not my dream house.

I was not living my dream life.

I walked home and wrote a heading in my journal

The Golden Ticket Life

I imagined someone handing me a Golden Ticket - it was not Willy Wonka in my day dream, it was a kind of God like person - face slightly obscured, I want to say wearing the white robes of the God of my Catholic youth but I think I may be rewriting history with that part.

God (ish) said:

here is your Golden Ticket - to your dream life, tell me, what does it look like?

I wrote it all down in my journal

Where is my dream house, how many bedrooms does it have?

What does the garden look like? What colour is the front door?

What car is in the driveaway?

Where do my children go to school?

How many hours do I work each week, in my dream life?

What is my dream job?

How does the dream version of me dress?

How does she wear her hair - how does she treat others around her?

How often does she spend time just being - relaxing, doing nothing?

What food does she eat?

How often does she have sex?

What legacy will she leave?

I sat for hours writing about my Golden Ticket life - the house in the sunshine, the calm confident woman who lived there, the car she drove, the clothes she wore - the way she felt and made others around her feel.

With every written word I realised that this life was within my reach.

All I had to was be clear on my desires and the actions I would take to receive them.

All creation comes from the feminine - feminine energy creates in the realm of the imagination and then the action we take (remember, action is masculine) brings the creation out from the unseen realm into the world of matter.

This is true of every creation from babies, to businesses to this book I am writing.

The feminine (in both men and women) creates in the unseen world of our imagination and the masculine manifests it in the 3D world.

An everyday example of this - let's take the creation of the table I am sitting at , right now

The design of the table was first seen in the minds eye, the imagination, of the creator, using their feminine energy. The shape, the colour, the materials used. All created without matter at this point - without a physical object. The table did not live in the 3D world, it lived in an unseen reality. How did it get from the feminine of the unseen to the masculine of the world of matter?

Action - *action* was taken to *build* the table, materials were sourced, bought, moulded to the desired shape etc.

The finished product, the table - is the 'child' of the two energies at work - feminine creative flow and masculine action.

So our Golden Ticket lives, our desires - they will require creativity and action.

The feminine and the masculine must work together to achieve this.

But first we must look at the fears of the inner child and how they are holding us back, as we walk the path to our Golden Ticket Life.

PART 3

Christmas Day 2022 ,

Tangier, Morocco

Friends, I did not stay still in the weeks that followed receiving my mammogram results in late November. I did not stay still at all.

If anything, I ran faster, harder and longer than I ever had before.

It was like someone let a ten year old loose with a credit card and the ability to book flights anywhere in the world. And that is exactly what I did.

In the space of a month I flew to Edinburgh, Cork, Venice and Madrid - I wrote feverishly every evening, walked for miles every day, performed rituals, read spiritual books - fasted for 72 hour periods more times than I care to remember - you name it, I tried it - anything to get back on my feet or that is what I thought I was trying to do.

In reality - I was doing anything to not stay still.

I had never felt so alone as when I boarded a flight to Morocco on the 25th of December 2022 - just under three months after my life monumentally fell to pieces.

In the final week, of what surely had been the very worst year of my life - I had spent Christmas Day alone, without either of my daughters, sitting in Gatwick airport, London, crying into a glass of water.

The longer I sat there, the worse I felt physically, flu like symptoms growing stronger with every passing hour. By the time I boarded the flight to Tangier I was almost delirious with exhaustion.

The plane landed at around 11pm on Christmas night, the excited holidaymakers clapped and cheered - smiling at each other .

Everyone so full of festive cheer, some flying home to see loved ones, others were taking a well deserved trip to the winter sun .

Everyone was smiling , laughing - excited for what lay ahead.

Everyone, that is, except me

I was sitting in my aisle seat, sweating profusely, head thumping, heart racing , my face flushed with the fever I had been carrying all afternoon as beads of sweat ran down my forehead.

Suddenly I began to cry

I must've looked as bad as I felt, as the handsome man sitting in the window seat beside me , turned to me, putting his hand gently on my arm and said in a thick accent

'everything is going to be ok'

I smiled weakly at him, nodding, praying he was right

When I reached my hotel a couple of hours later, I could barely lift my head up to speak to the pretty receptionist who was checking me in - there seemed to be a problem with the booking that I had made that afternoon, but I did not have the energy to engage with her about it. I just smiled and nodded in between putting my head on the cold reception desk in a somewhat vain attempt to cool myself down.

Eventually the receptionist touched my arm and I looked up to see her holding out my room key

Respite at last - even if it was just for a few hours.

I stripped naked as soon as I closed the room door behind me and lay on top of the duvet with the air con blasting

Drifting in and out of consciousness , sleep came, at last - as did the strange lucid dreams I had been having on and off for the past three months .

The next morning I woke at 11am , bedsheets soaked in sweat - the fever still gripping my body.

I wrestled between lying in bed all day or cooling down in the sea - I knew it was close by as I heard the waves when I arrived in the early hours

The cool sea won me over and I got dressed, wincing in pain with every move of my aching body.

I walked tentatively down to the deserted sandy beach and sat alone on the sand , tears streaming down my face as I watched the waves crash onto the shore

December 26th, 2022

Hundreds of miles from my daughters, from my friends, from anyone I knew

Completely and utterly alone.

Scared, sad, confused and feeling more physically unwell than I ever had in my life.

I sat there on the sand in a dream like state and spoke out loud

Please help me, I will do whatever it takes to get back on my feet
Please show me a way out of this mess

hot tears streamed down my face as I wailed and sobbed like a child in full blown tantrum mode

Please, please, please help me I cried over and over, eventually laying down on the sand overcome with despair.

And as the waves crashed against the shore I heard two words, crystal clear in my body.

Resist nothing

And all at once I felt that same peaceful feeling wash over my body again.

Resist Nothing.

I did not know it then, but those two words would change my life.

They would become the anchor I needed , to finally turn my life around once and for all.

Once again, the spiritual intelligence of my body had spoken - and this time, I was determined to listen.

OUR BASELINE BLUEPRINT
THE CHILD WITHIN

What fears are holding me back?

My biggest fear and my biggest desire are one and the same.

I want to be seen.

We all want to be seen.

This desire is inherent in all human beings - firstly in childhood, we want our parents to see us, to acknowledge us and to love us unconditionally. Unfortunately most of us did not grow up in that environment, one where unconditional love was the order of the day. I have two wonderful daughters, I could sit here and tell you until I am blue in the face, that I love them unconditionally - but the truth is, they do not know that until they *feel* that love.

I have no doubt in my *mind* that my mother loved me unconditionally. When I told her about the abuse in my childhood, at the age of just twenty one years old, she swore me to secrecy from telling my siblings, and I complied because subconsciously - all I wanted, was for her to still love me, despite what I had told her. I wanted her to be happy so I did as she asked - would she still have loved me if I had told my family in her lifetime? I believe she would have, I really do, but I did not know that consciously at the time. I was conditioned into behaving the way my parents wanted me to behave since before I could talk. So I did what she asked me to do. My inner child was running the show.

Most of us were conditioned to be who our parents wanted us to be - whilst not being seen for who we actually were.

(Once again, this is not a parent bashing book - I am now that parent, trying my best. You are no doubt about it, also trying your best. I say this to bring awareness to the situation - with awareness comes change)

All children want to be seen, just seen in order to feel safe - this means for the "good" and the "bad" parts of their personality. But we praise them for the good and so these are the parts they try to show most - and into the shadows go the "bad" traits.

This is something I am acutely aware of now with my youngest daughter.

It shows up in the most ordinary of places - a few weeks ago Frances and I were baking cupcakes (I still bake cupcakes, just not five dozen at a time) , when I tied her hair up away from her face, in a loose bun at the top of her head. I wear my hair like this most days (unless I am going somewhere fancy, you know, like the supermarket etc...) and remarked to Frances at the time, without thinking - *oh look we are twins! You are wearing a cute bun like mama*

Frances found this hilarious as I have very dark hair while she has pure blonde hair, she giggled loudly when I said it - but then I saw a look of discomfort flash across her face as she tried to position the hair tie to a more comfortable spot. I fixed it for her and told her she could take the hair tie out as soon as we had finished baking. I did not think anything more of it.

The next day, Frances was standing in front of the mirror as I brushed her hair for school, when she asked me to put her hair up in a bun. I obliged without thinking about the day before , but as I watched her in the mirror the same look of discomfort flashed across her face again.

Frances, do you like wearing your hair like this? I asked

She did not say yes, instead she replied *"its cute, like your hair"* and I felt my heart sink as I realised the impact my flippant words had on her the day before. I quickly brushed the bun out and asked Frances to show me how she would like to wear her hair to school - explaining the importance of not doing anything that makes us feel uncomfortable just to make others happy.

Frances wants to be seen, she asked me to fix her hair in that way so that I would see her and praise her, just like I had done the day before. I have to be vigilant in my awareness of my own words around her at all times. My first job as her mother is to let her know I can see her - all of her.

My initial realisation of this desire to be seen had come the summer before - when I watched Frances play in the park, one day, with a few little girls she had made friends with in Portugal. Four little girls all filled with mischief and wonder running about a playpark in the sunshine. Just finding their feet and testing the world around them with their emerging personalities. One of the girls stood out from the group immediately.

She was louder than the rest, taller, more rambunctious - she just seemed - in a word - *more*

And what I noticed straight away was that she was almost "too much" more for the children around her.

I sat watching them all interacting in the park, paying particular attention to this one child - wondering why she was behaving the way she was. I could see the other girls growing frustrated with her, at times, overbearing personality and then it struck me -

She just wants to be seen.

This little girl was overflowing with energy, she did not know what to do with it and her energetic body was screaming out

Can you see me? Tell me you can see me!

I wondered how often she had been told to quieten down, stop shouting, stop running - stop being herself.

A little while later, as the group ran over to me for snacks I made sure to simply acknowledge her - to literally just tell her I could see her.

I said the words - *I see you waiting patiently for a snack*

Later I told her - *I see you getting upset when you can't go first on the climbing frame.*

No praise or punishment.

I see you.

Just an acknowledgement that she is seen.

This is what we are all looking for in life.

I first began writing this book in 2021, for that same simple reason. I want people to see me - to see me for who I truly am. I want to say this is me - Alyson Larkin, these are the things that have happened to me and these are the things that I have done to others. These are my redeeming features and these are my flaws.These are the thoughts and theories I have based on the stories I tell myself - some of them you may agree with some of them you may not.

I spent most of my life hiding the real me - in truth, Tim was the first person to truly see me. On our very first date, in Valetta in the spring of 2021 he told me he could see me with one simple statement :

' Ah you're actually interested in people … that's what it is … that's why this happens. You look people right in the eye and ask them how they are … for most people it's just lip service, but you actually care'

I knew the very time I met Tim that he would not let me hide - he was determined to look right at me.

I had spent the year prior to that conversation, looking people right in the eye in 1-2-1 coaching spaces, while they told me their worst fears and the stories that caused them the most shame

I had heard the stories of women who cheated on their husbands, who secretly resented their children, who had been raped, abused, cheated on, left behind.

I heard from men who no longer felt attracted to their wives, who hated what they saw in the mirror, who had hurt others and who were terrified of letting people down.

I looked them right in the eye and let them know that I could see them. And that they were safe to voice these stories.

But I had never let anyone really see me - and now this man was looking at me, deeper than anyone had ever looked at me before and I was fucking terrified.

I had been in therapy following the ending of my marriage in 2020 and had learned lots about why I was who I was and how my childhood had shaped me. I had looked myself in the eye - in the mirror and acknowledged the person I had created without conscious knowledge.

But now I had to let *someone else* in to look at me too?

Really, really in. To see the *real* me ...

I was scared - but I took a leap with Tim.

Over the course of our relationship that followed, I opened myself up to him wider than I ever had with anyone before.

I did not just get physically naked with this man - I got spiritually naked too.

I told him in minute detail about *all* the memories I had of the molestation - I told him what had happened physically, how it affected me psychologically, and how it felt in my body to say those words out loud. I told him about the nightmares I had suffered from about the abuse, for most of my life.

I told him how I had faked every orgasm with every man I had ever slept with - how my body had been in the room but my innate sexuality had been fragmented off long before, in my bed as a child.

But the most open thing I told him was that I had lived most of my life in a state of fear - fear that I was broken, tainted, disgusting - warped in some way by what my abuser did.

I let Tim see me.

The first time we slept together I had an earth shattering orgasm - real, strong, powerful ... terrifying.

This man could not only see me... he could feel me too.

Soon after I began to experience trauma release almost every time we had sex. The first time Tim massaged my G-spot I felt a tidal wave of grief rush to the surface - an ocean of sadness. It hit me like a tsunami and I wailed and sobbed ike a child in his arms. I had no idea that my body had such depth of feeling.

Then came the noises and shaking - demonic sounding energy, screaming and screeching followed almost every time I climaxed. I was horrified the first time it happened - It felt like I was being posessed.

My repressed emotions were being released through my voice and through violent shaking - it was like the emotions had morphed into some kind of entity that was being purged from my body during orgasm.

This lasted for months and the thing that terrified me most was that Tim could tell when I was trying to contain it. He would say to me time and time again - *stop holding it in, just let it happen.* He remained grounded and strong throughout, creating the container for my energy to flow.

Ever since I began meditating, on the advice of my therapist in 2020, I had experienced visions when in a meditative state - but they did not even closely compare to the visions I would experience during orgasm. Sometimes I would come out with random sentences that made no sense to me or Tim at the time - but within a few days I realised the words were clear messages guiding me down a path. My body was speaking to me.

I was lowkey embarrassed about it all - I spoke with Ed, my therpaist, who told me that sexual energy and God (spirituality) are closely linked - this was not the first time he had heard of stories like mine. He told me to always trust the messages I received - that they were coming from beyond this world. He said I was blessed to receive them.

I did not feel blessed - this was another 'thing' that made me different, had I not been through enough sexually, now I was seeing God everytime I climaxed... bit dramatic, hey?

I asked myself time and time again was I making it all up in my mind? Perhaps it was the child version of me who was traumatised so horrifically just looking for a something to distract her during sex?

(I am not rulling this explanation out entirely- I hold onto all of my theories on this lightly,)

But the visions kept coming true and the messages continued to show me the way forward.

And with every orgasmic release I noticed something else. I could feel intense sexual energy surging through my body everytime I even *thought* about having sex - it was nothing like I had ever felt before. Of course, I had felt sexual urges all of my adult life - but nothing like this. And it wasn't just when I was thinking about sex (or having sex) but when I was eating enjoyable food, or listening to music. My friends laughed when I told them I was worried one day I would orgasm just from drinking a glass of cold sparkling water. It was like every sensual pleasure was affecting my body in ways I had never felt previously.

The trauma release was turning on every single cell in my body.

It felt Divine. There was something untouched under all the trauma, something completely pure and clear - it was like a coming home to myself.

I started to wonder if maybe the very place in which I was so horrendously wounded in childhood, my sexual energy, was also the key to not just releasing the trapped energies but to rediscovering the spiritual wisdom of the body.

Could orgasm and the evolution of consciousness go hand in hand? I meditated on this for months and began to guide my clients through using orgasm for release.

But throughout it all I had a fear hidden, deep, deep down inside that one day all of this would be too much for Tim. I would make jokes about him leaving on account of my witchiness.

It was a self fulfilling prophecy - because of course, when Tim left, I told myself I had been right all along - I was too broken, too tainted, too weird. And my inner child who was in there hiding, in the shadows of my subconscious, took over.

I became that ten year old child again, filled with shame and fear.

And that was when I began to realise what my inner child's personality was based on. A paradox - the desire of the little girl with the big ideas who wants to be seen and loved - and in my shadow - a lifetime of feeling not worthy, not good enough. Broken by my past.

Like a thousand tiny paper cuts this feeling of not being good enough did not just come from one single incident - although I would be naive to think the main trauma of my childhood did not play a part. And it did, of course it did - but it was not the *only* reason I had always felt this way.

It was every time I got it "wrong" - every failed test in school, the realisation I was not as pretty as the class beauty, the fact my best friend growing up, had an incredible singing voice while I sounded like a cat being strangled. The times my mother, trying to give her attention to five children, did not listen to me instead giving her attention to one of my brothers or my sister.

Desperate to be seen - whilst simultaneously terrified of being seen in case I did not measure up.

Over the years I used less than beneficial ways to try and prove my worth to myself and others - I exaggerated my achievements, full of grandiosity and bravado.

I judged others, holding them up to ridiculously high standards, then berated them in my mind when they 'failed' to meet the standards I had silently set. I projected the shame of my unworthiness outwards as judgement.

I had relationships with men who were already in realtionship - happy to be the 'other woman' as that meant I did not have to get too close to anyone and to somehow, without conscious thought, prove to myself that I was more desirable than their spouses. My ego always provided vailid reasons for doing so.

Desperate to be good enough. Desperate to be seen. My wounded inner child running the show.

The Universe does not take too kindly to those who walk that path, my life was filled with chaos throughout that time.

I take full responsibility for the havoc I brought into my life in my twenties and thirties - but this past year, I have learned to give myself grace too.

Because I realised that if I am going to face my fears in talking openly about what happened to me in childhood, in what was done to me by another - I must also face the shame of what I , myself, have done to others.

And if I forgive the actions of those who have hurt me, which I do - I must also forgive myself.

It has been said, by a mind far greater than mine, that the tortured becomes the torturer - and this is for sure the path I followed for much of my life.

The shame I carried inside moulded me into becoming a person who was not walking the path of a good life. It was in looking at that shame - and my own actions that I was able to change my path.

(By the way - I am not saying this has some kinda holier than thou, born again messiah who has found God and repented for all her sins … I am human like everyone else, I can still be the biggest asshole in the room when I let myself slip. And I do, frequently)

What I have noticed - the more I actively work on staying in my body and not my mind, is that my body physically nudges me when I am falling back into old habits.

Literally - like I will feel a shift, a jerk in my body, if I say something that is not kind, or not beneficial. If I find myself in a situation where I am aggravated in anyway by something outside of myself - a person or a situation, I have this little internal checkpoint that stops me. It's a *feeling* in my body - which I could only reach by feeling all the other feelings first.

My first thought when I find myself being nudged for looking out there, to the other - *this is here to show me something about myself not **that** person or **this** situation - this is about me, and the path I am walking.*

What am I learning? Why is this happening?

What have *I* done to cause this situation to happen in my life?

I am the only person in my Universe, everyone outside of me is a mirror for me to look in. If I do not see a clean mirror then it is because my perception is clouded - not because of the situation or person in front of me. If another person, who is not walking the path for their highest good, somehow ends up on my path, causing a situation I do not like, then the first thing I ask myself is how did this person end up on my path? What is going on with me that has drawn this situation towards me.

It is always, always because I have stepped off the path of Least Resistance.

But I give myself grace when I mess up too - because I know it is my inner child running the show. When things seem difficult, I ask myself the same question over and over - how old is the version of me who is walking the path today?

My personality was created through the eyes of a little girl who was taught to lie by omission - as a child, in my own bed, in my own home, where I should have been more safe than anywhere else in the world. I lied by omission by not telling my mother what was happening at the time - because I knew it was wrong . I did not know how to tell her so I learned to lie instead.

I then spent most of my life lying. To others yes, over the years - but mostly to myself.

My personality was created on omitting the full truth, and the day I realised this, I felt soul crushing shame - much like the shame I felt when I was first molested.

I looked back on my life and saw every half truth I had ever told

Every time I bit my tongue instead of saying how I really felt

Every time I had manipulated a situation to get what I wanted - and this had happened a lot.

I lost friends due to my untrustworthiness , I made enemies due to my actions.

When I told one of my brothers about the sexual abuse,initially, he did not believe me - the first words out of his mouth were - *but Aly you exaggerate everything, you always have.*

I told Tim afterwards, *he is right you know - he is right. But I am telling the truth now - and no one will believe me.*

I was the girl who cried wolf.

I said earlier in this book that I believed that I had had more adversity than others in my life time - but I can also see where I invited that adversity in.

Where I created chaos, unknowingly, to distract myself from my feeling of unworthiness.

And once again, I asked myself over and over -

"How old was the version of you who behaved that way, Aly"

The answer more often than not came back -

ten years old - the year I was abused

fifteen years old - the year I consciously remembered the abuse after five years of complete memory loss of it (which I found out later in therapy, is very common)

Well rounded, grounded, stable grown ups do not lie, they do not omit the truth, they do not exaggerate ... this is the behaviour of children who did not get a chance to grow up in a safe environment.

Many women I have coached have told me, over the years about times when they spent money and did not tell their husbands, for fear of being 'told off'. They have downplayed the amount they spent or hidden it altogether - out of a disproprtionate (and this is the important word here, this is not women who are in any danger from their spouses) fear that they have done something wrong. More often than not, the same women have told me about times when they felt shame in their childhood due to their father's being disappointed in them for something and how they had to work hard at not upsetting him. They then created a personality that revolved around earning their father's affection. That good girl behaviour, the perfect persona is then carried into their marriage and creates a situation where a lot of women do not feel safe to be fully naked with their husband.

I created a false personality, based on the interactions I had in childhood

With my Father
With Money
With the Catholic God
With my Mother
With my Sexual nature
With my Creativity

And in truth, that personality for most of my twenties and thirties was not very nice. She told half truths and exaggerated stories. She drank too much, gossiped too much and judged outside of herself a lot.

The people who judge the most are the ones with the most shame in their bodies - we just project that shame outwards as well as internalising it.

I should know - I spent years doing it.

This book is the third book I have written - the two previous attempts were read by a handful of people and then did not see the light of day. Despite a publishing offer and praise from all who read it - I was simply too afraid to release my writing - my fears were greater than my desires.

The only way to alchemise fear into pure power is by doing the thing that scares you most.

This is how we move from the lower self to the higher self - through the middle passage.

All action happens in the present.

How am I overcoming my fear of being seen for my writing? You are reading it here… You can see me.

It feels scary … and powerful all at once.

When we have sat with ourselves and asked the first two questions in recognising our path:

Who am I ?

What do I desire?

We must then , acknowledge the fears that are holding us back from taking the action to fully receive those desires.

This is where the magic happens - the fun part. We get to voice our fears out loud and in doing so, we realise they are, more often than not, not even real.

And even if they could be real , the next question I ask all of my clients is -

So what?

So what if your biggest fear comes true?

What happens if and when it does?

Will you hide under a duvet and never come out again?

Or will you look your fears straight in the face and conquer them?

My all time favourite thing to ask my clients, when they tell me they are afraid _____ (insert fear here) will happen:

So. Fucking. What?

Nearly every time I get the same reply

Laughter. Followed by the realisation that, if that fear did come true - they would not get under the duvet and never come back out again

My biggest fear was that Tim, the only man I had ever let see the real me, would leave

And he did!

Guess what? I did go under my duvet, but I got back out again.

I stood back up.

Fear lives in the shadow - the ONLY way to eradicate it is to bring it out from the shadows into the light.

What are you most afraid of? Write it down - and then ask yourself if that fear came true - what would happen next? What would you do? How would you react?

Write it down - then let it go.

Ok, enough about fears- let's talk about the power of clear desire - much more fun!

What do you most desire? What does your dream life look like?

How fat apart is your life now and your dream life in the future?What action must you take to alchemise one into the other?

How do we alchemise fear into power?

I spent years understanding all of this cognitively but the actual actions - speaking out, being seen, screaming my anger out at the top of my lungs - I ran from those actions. Time and time again. Until that phone call, in October 2022 , that brought my life crashing down around my ears *forcing* me to face my fears *through* the body .

In the body - the scariest place I have ever lived (and I grew up on the mean streets of Greenock) is in my body - WITH my feelings.

One of the most terrifying experiences I ever had of being fully in my body, was while sitting outside a beautiful air bnb in southern Europe, on a patio overlooking the Mediterranean Sea. It was around 9am, I was sitting at the table with a cup of coffee, listening to the sound of soft waves lapping against the shore a few metres from my bedroom door, the sun was not yet high enough to be too hot. The surroundings were as tranquil and as postcard perfect as you could possibly imagine. I closed my eyes and began the process of emptying myself of thought - when I felt the strongest sense of fear inside my chest. It was so strong that I immediately opened my eyes wondering if there was something dangerous nearby ... (this was in a beautiful resort, I was staying in the last house right on the sea front - the most dangerous thing I had encountered since arriving was a stray cat that would meaow at the door some evenings while I sat writing in the front room. The owner had told me the people on the resort had nicknamed the cat Gary. To my knowledge, Gary was not dangerous, I felt pretty certain I could defend myself against a cat should the situation arise.) I was alone, my heart was pounding in my chest, fear gripped my body and I had no idea why. I stood up and walked towards the end of my little garden, through the hole in the fence on the perimeter of the property and headed straight for the sea. I got into the shallow, clear water, ducked my head under for a second then stood waiting for the feeling to pass. If anything, it seemed to be getting worse.

I stayed with the feeling, I did not try and attach a story to it, I just let the fear rise, knowing it needed to go somewhere - somewhere outside of me. Suddenly I knew I needed to move the fear - I began punching the water, smacking my hands down on the surface really hard and fast, then I began to shout.

I want my mum, I want my mum, I want my mum

the shouting lasted for two or three minutes - punching and screaming throughout. There was no single memory attached - just a child, trapped in the body of a woman, screaming for the person who brought her into this world.

I let her scream, I let her punch the water - and then I let her go. Afterwards I felt like I could run up a mountain - the feeling of light was unbelievable.

This is how I alchemised the fear, long held in my body, into power.

I did it through breath work, through silent meditation, menstruation and orgasm - but most of all - through taking ACTION to change.

At times it felt like I was dying - I was

A version of me was dying to be reborn with every action I took.

The first action - slow down

The second action - resist nothing

And then I asked myself the three questions

Who am I ?
What do I desire?
What fears are holding me back?

With the release of this writing, with the digital programme that follows it - (complete with me facing my other worst fear … talking on video for nine whole sessions, pray for me)… I am taking the action needed , to alchemise the fear I created in childhood , into the power that is waiting for me on the other side of that very fear.

The power to receive my true desires ...

Let's Go!

ΔΔΔ

LEAST RESISTANCE - AS A WAY OF LIFE.

July 2023

Seville, Spain.

I spent ten days in Morocco, from Chistmas Day 2022 until early 2023. For the first five days I sat under the same tree in a park near my hotel, meditating in silence. I would sit there for hours in the warm Moroccan sunshine, sitting still just like my body had instructed me to.

On the first day nothing out of the ordinary happened...but the next day, out of nowhere my body began to spasm and contort, just like it had in bed with Tim. This happened a few times over the coming days and then the contortions began to take over my face, twisting it involuntary completely out of my control. This was new and extremely frightening - my jaw would shake with such intensity I was afraid I would cause permanent damage. There was a version of me, in the background, during these episodes, terrified, hearing my late mother's voice say "if the wind changes your face will stay like that" … good thing there was no wind in Tangier at that time of year.

But, in truth, underneath the fear, I also had an inner knowing throughout, that my body was just doing something that it deperately needed to do.

Releasing a lifetime of tension, stress and trauma.

(perhaps more than one lifetime, but thats a story for another book)

It was under that tree in Vila Harris Park, that I first learned to release the trauma somatically from my body through meditation.

It was there that I learned the true meaning of resisting nothing. I had to simply allow my body to twist and turn with the release, in public, under a tree, completely alone.

Over the six months that followed, I would have many, many more instances where I would physically release all that I had been carrying inside - through breathwork, meditation, menstruation and orgasm.

I would shake, scream and shout as I finally set free the versions of myself that had been buried decades before. In one particular occasion I lay on the floor of my apartment during a breath work session and saw the face of my abuser above me. I could smell his breath and feel the sick warm feeling of him being too close as I finally reacted in the way my body had wanted to some thirty years before - I screamed, punched and kicked with all of my might - shouting at the top of my lungs over and over

No no no no no no - stop that stop that stop that

Finally I let that ten year old be free - I let her be heard as I screamed and punched the floor while kicking the empty air above me. My physical body was in England, in 2023 a grown woman - my psyche, my fragmented consciousness was ten years old, lying in her childhood bedroom in Scotland fighting for her life.

I brought her to the surface and I let her know - she would survive, she would not die, she was free to react the way she wanted to - I would make sure she was safe. The physical exhaustion afterwards was so deep that I could not get out of bed for a few days - I had been carrying that little girl around for decades, no wonder I always felt so heavy.

Throughout the months I worked on my trauma release somatically, I followed the two words I had heard on the beach in Tangier religiously :

Resist Nothing

Everything that was put on my path I saw as a nod from the Universe - a Divine signal guiding me to where I needed to be. If I felt any resistance, any fear whatsoever - I immediately sat in silence to hear the spiritual wisdom of my body. I asked my womb what the next step was and follwed what I heard - no matter what my body told me to do.

And then slowly, almost imperceptibly, the magic started happening …

In resisting nothing I realised I was gaining everything.

All of my desires began flowing to me.

My friend Sarah was the first to notice outside of me - she said to me one morning

Aly, have you realised that you say something out loud and then within a few days it actually happens... whatever you ask for you get?

I had begun to see it too and had wondered if my mind was playing tricks on me - did I really have this much power?

Quietly, quietly, my life started picking up again, I would wake in the morning feeling excited for the day ahead , my creative juices were flowing unlike ever before. I began a new coaching programme for women - *The Way of the Women,* where I walked women through their own versions of least resistance. And the changes in their lives were astronomical.

I dipped my toe back into in person coaching - but this time we weren't just working cognitively through behaviour change, we were shifting energy, physically.

I was alchemising my pain into power and passing the lessons I had learned along the way, onto the women I coached.

When my long term client Rena, arrived from Canada , in May to spend a week doing trauma release work with me, she told me that she had been in touch with Tim (who was also her business coach when we first met) and had arranged a dinner with him during her trip.

I smiled and told her I was happy that they were finally meeting in person, and I meant it - I really did. But there was also a version of me in there who still felt fear - I had spent months grieving the loss of our relationship and had finally got to a place where I could function with a semblance of normality, only to be faced with hearing his name again.

The grown up, coach and mentor version of me was truly happy that Rena was able to meet Tim in person but the heartbroken, very feminine in her *feelings* - version of me was still trying to come to terms with living without him. I still missed him terribly, every bit as much as I did in the beginning. Yes, I could see the power of what those months of turmoil had shown me but Tim was not just my partner, he was my best friend and I missed him so much it still hurt physically. We had barely spoken more than a few words to each other in eight months. Much like the sudden death of my mother , he was in my life one day and gone completely the next. Without any solid reason. The abandonment wound I had felt from my mother all of my life, her inability to protect me in my own home as a child , her dismissal of my pain when I told her of the abuse year later - all of this - abandonment and dismissal - had been playing out again in adulthood for months - a different story, the same pain.

As much as I felt grateful for the life lessons I was learning - I was still just a woman with a broken heart.

A myriad of emotions ran through me when I heard Rena would be meeting with Tim - but I smiled and repeated my favourite two words

Least Resistance.

I felt like the Universe was really putting me to the test - *ok Aly let's see how much you can follow the free flowing path that's put in front of you each day...*

I was up for the challenge …

Then a few days later Tim's name appeared on my phone, a curt, emotionless message - inviting me to the dinner - obligatory rather than through personal preference.

Every part of my ego screamed no, as I froze in fear, reading the message. I could not have dinner with this man. No way!

Least resistance went out the window.

But I knew I would have to accept or I would be going against everything I had been coaching Rena through for months - how could I tell her to resist nothing if I resisted this dinner invitation?

My ego tried to come up with a million different reasons as to why least resistance did not work in *this* particular situation. But my body kept repeating ... resist nothing

Damn least resistance …

I accepted the awkward invite and so, found myself sitting opposite Tim a few nights later. We made it through a terse few hours, eating and talking through old times. Every now and again catching each others eyes in an in-joke no one else would understand.

I did not know that pleasure and pain could sit so close together. But I made it through. I resisted nothing.

I am healed, I thought afterwards … *I am healed.*

(Insert narrators voice … she was not healed, reader - she was definitely not healed.)

Of course I wasn't - and two days later when Rena met up with Tim for a coffee, without me, I cried like a child for hours.

Decades old wounds surfaced - *every* instance of abandonment I had felt in childhood came rushing to the forefront of my consciousness as I lay in bed sobbing, heart broken and grief stricken.

And it was then, that I came to see what had happened for the gift it truly was, a chance to comfort the original wounded child within me.

This was not about the abandonment I felt from Tim in present day, but about the abandonment I had originally felt, decades before, in my parents home. It was about *all* the times I had felt that way.

Tim had refused to see me for months, refused to acknowledge my existence - but this was a *reopening* of the original wound - the refusal of my parents to *see* me for who I really was in childhood.

And because I was not seen, because no one looked at me closely enough, no one saw the shame and confusion behind my eyes and so the abuse continued.

I realised then, the fear I had been carrying for months , was, if Tim could not see me, then I would be hurt, horrifically - just like I was as a child.

It felt like I would die if I was not seen - just like it did all those years ago.

Once again, I did not rush that little girl version of me to let go, I sat with her as she cried all the tears that had been stored inside.

Grief wracked my body - but I let it come up to be seen, by *me*.

I could see me - and that was enough.

When Rena left the UK a few days later, I booked into a beautiful five star hotel and lay in bed for three days releasing the fear through my body - finally.

A few days later I packed up the very last of Tim's things from my apartment and sent them to his mums, along with a gift I had bought for him a few months earlier. A signed copy of a book his paternal grandfather had written in the 60's, that I had spent over a year searching for.

I wanted to leave him with a gift of love.

I put a handwritten note in with the book - saying goodbye and thanking Tim for all he had done for me in the time I had known him.

And I truly meant it - resisting nothing, accepting my reality had given me the presence to understand - It is not what happens to us, but how we tell the story, what we do with the lessons that we have learned, that truly matters.

I had spent nine long months raging against the injustice of what had happened between Tim and I, but I had forgotten one thing throughout, I was not that ten year old child anymore. I was not that girl who was abandoned in her time of need. I was a grown woman - who could never be abandoned , not by Tim, not by anyone. I had lived most of my adult life through the lens of that traumatised little girl and it had taken this heartbreak in adulthood to really, fully show me that this lens was simply untrue.

A few weeks later I booked a flight to Seville in southern Spain, to spend ten days in a beautiful, spacious, modern apartment, smack bang in the city centre where I would finish writing this book.

I arrived on Monday the 10th of July - bouncing along in the intense sunshine, pulling my new pink suitcase. Like an excited child, ready to explore this new city, write to my hearts content and eat as much paella as humanly possible.

Vamanos !

My apartment was located a two minute walk from a beautiful Catholic Church, where I had decided in advance, I would begin my day, each morning, by listening to the Mass in Spanish. Despite having turned my back on organised religion many years before, I still love to visit churches and sacred sites. I never anchor myself to any particular religion, rather just going where my feet take me - but the Catholic Churches I have visited on my travels always feel extra special - it is a connection I have with my mother that I will always cherish.

The first day I sat in the church of Mary Magdalene, I was overcome with emotion and sobbed quietly throughout the mass. It was like part of me knew I was at the end of this nine month journey and that a new version of me was in the process of being birthed. When the service was over I knelt on the little pew in the penultimate row and spoke to a God I truly believe lives inside of us and does not limit himself to bricks and mortar establishments. But I was in his symbolic home and had something to tell Him.

I am ready.

Please show me the next step I will take after this book is complete.

I want nothing more than to love and be loved, to be married and have a family - with Eilidh & Frances and more babies in my arms.

Please send the man who will lead me on this path.

I am ready.

I blessed myself , stood and genuflected before the altar and turned to leave. In my minds eye I could see my mum nodding in approval as I smiled to myself walking out into the beautiful Spanish sunshine . I may not follow the Catholic Religion - but I respect the rituals and rules of any house I enter, my mother taught me that. I blew a kiss up in to the sky, hoping she could catch it - her energy is somewhere out there in the ether, of that I am sure. Then I practically skipped the whole way back to my apartment, excited for the days ahead.

I spent the next week indulging my inner child daily - I slept late every morning and ate the most amazing ice cream I have ever tasted, from a little takeaway near my apartment, that I visited every evening, after a walk around the city. I watched comedy shorts on YouTube and danced wildly (for wildly, read naked) in my spacious kitchen to 80's music.

I did indeed eat paella and patatas bravas of course, along with ceviche and lots of other local dishes that delighted my taste buds with every bite.

I felt a light that I had never felt before in Sevlille - I smiled at strangers everywhere I went and became a regular in the cafes and restaurants near to my apartment. I practised my high school Spanish that I had not had a chance to try out for years and with each passing day I felt my strength return. I began, after nine long months, to feel excited for the future.

I spoke with friends daily, telling them about my writing, my ideas, my plans - the world was my oyster and I was determined to live every single day to the fullest from here on in.

The Saturday after I arrived, I decided to go for lunch in my new local, a traditional eatery with the loveliest waiting staff who always gave me the best recommendations from the specials menu each time I visited.

I spent longer than usual curling my hair and picking out a pretty outfit - an off the shoulder, blue flowery dress that reached to my ankles but had a thigh high slit down the side. Maybe a bit overdressed for lunch on my own on a random Saturday but I was in full feminine flow from writing all week and was channeling that artistic energy through to my outfit.

The feminine desires to be seen.

I slicked on red lip gloss, sprayed some Chanel and perched my oversized sunglassess on top of my perfectly curled hair - before walking out into the warm sunshine, ready for the day ahead.

I decided, when I got to the restaurant, to sit outside even although the sun was high in the sky and temperatures were in the early 40's. Seville is well equipped for this level of heat and the canopy outside the restaurant provided plenty of shade and an intermittent spritz of cool misty water every few seconds , which I loved. This was now the fourth or fifth time I had been to this particular place and had soon realised, in my previous visits, that the main thoroughfare was a magnet for local homeless people begging for spare change. When I had noticed this on my first visit I made a mental note to go to an ATM so that I would be able to give some money during my stay - much like the late Queen of England I never carry cash, but I wanted to give something back to the people of this beautiful city. What better way than to help those most in need.

I had been sidetracked by cathedrals and delicious ice cream in the week since I arrived and was annoyed that I had not managed to withdraw any cash yet ,when, a few minutes after I had been seated, I was approached by an older gentleman. He looked to be in his late 50's early 60's, and smiled shyly as he held out a cap and a note in English, asking for any spare change to take back to his family. I shook my head and tried in my rudimentary Spanish to convey that I had no cash on me - when suddenly I was struck with an idea.

I took my phone out of my little orange rattan bag and quickly typed into google translate

Can I buy you lunch from here instead?

When I showed him the words on my screen he stared at me without speaking - just as the waitress was walking past. I explained to her, in

English , what I had proposed to the man and she shook her head, telling me they did not provide takeaway.

She went on to explain further - I could for sure, buy the man lunch, but he would have to sit at my table with me to eat it.

I quickly realised, I once again, had the opportunity to spend some time with a stranger who could become a friend.

The ebb and flow of the Universe.

Like a spiral, we come back to the same stories time and time again.

I asked the waitress to explain what she had just said to my new amigo, invite him to my table for me and to please, bring another menu.

I soon found out the man spoke no English at all - zero, zilch … nada - I tried my best at small talk in Spanish , momentarily discombobulated, wondering how we would get through the meal…

Soy Escocesa

I said smiling and nodding - having no idea really, why I felt the need to explain to this man, my Scottish roots -

But somehow this broke the ice, as he rubbed his arms in the universal sigh language for cold and said *ah frio, frio*

I don't think he had ever been to Scotland, but he knew that it's cold there apparently!

I smiled back, nodding enthusiastically and the friendship was cemented.

Who needs words - we could just sit together, eating and smiling.

Energy speaks louder than words ever will.

Before we even had the chance to order - another homeless man approached our table, a friend of my new friend. This gentleman had a definite air of long ago held aristocracy that I knew could never truly be taken from him, regardless of his current life situation. He was dressed in clothes that, once upon a time, would not have looked out of place in a fine eating establishment or a Sunday morning in church. The suit was worn and dirty but in its heyday im sure it was well looked after. He spoke in rapid Spanish to the other man who gestured towards me, I assumed, explaining to him, that this slightly strange Scottish woman had invited him for lunch .

Spanish señor número dos, nodded at me, seemingly in approval. I had passed some kinda test by the look of it. Phew!

I pulled another chair up from the table next to us and pointed at it for the new attendee to take a seat.

Let's turn this lunch into a small party.

The bemused waitress returned with another menu and a quizzical look in my direction as she took our orders. The three of us sat in comfortable silence together while we waited for our food to arrive and then spent the next thirty minutes or so making hand gestures towards our plates and speaking to each other intermittently in broken English/Spanish … it was lovely and slightly strange but somehow very fitting for this new life I was about to embark on.

Who better to help me celebrate my death and rebirth than two lovely Spanish men who did not speak a word of English?

We finished our lunch and I motioned to the waitress to please bring the bill. I thanked the two gentlemen for joining me - they nodded back, still looking slightly bemused, repeating *gracias* over and over until I was around the corner.

The city centre was getting busier and as I walked through the main thoroughfare, deciding what flavour of ice cream to buy,   I smiled to myself at the randomness of what had just happened.

I was meandering along with a little spring in my step, taking in all the sights and sounds just as I had done every day, when something caught my attention out of the corner of my eye.

A teenage boy walking along had dropped something from his back pack and was continuing down the street unknowingly:

Excuse me , excuse me- I called trying desperately to remember how to grab someone's attention in Spanish, just as he turned around. I picked his t-shirt off the ground and handed it to him smiling, when then strangest thing happened.

He took the bright, white t-shirt from my hand and firmly shook it out, unfurling it in front of me

As I heard the words very clearly in my body

he will wave a white flag, be prepared

I shook my head in confusion and the Spanish boy mirrored the same look of confusion back to me - it was as if time had stopped for a moment. He was there as some kind of messenger and I felt that we both knew this on some level - but neither of us knew who had sent the message.

Or what the message meant.

But I had heard the words loud and clear - part of me wondered if he had heard them too.

I smiled and nodded at him in acceptance - as he turned and left just as quickly as he had arrived.

I walked home bemused, pondering the white t-shirt.

Oh - and in case you were wondering … I had triple chocolate ice cream in the end. Still my favourite.

In the wee hours of the morning, the next day, in that very special moment between sleep and wake - when it feels like we are in-between two worlds, I heard the message again.

He will wave a white flag, tomorrow.

This time, a face accompanied the words as they flooded through my body.

A face belonging to someone I knew very well.

Tim.

I shook my head and brought myself out into the world of consciousness, fully awake and slightly pissed off.

A white flag, I scoffed to myself, from Tim of all people.

Definitely not.

It was Sunday the 16th of July, Seville was basking in a heat wave - I had never felt anything like it in my life. The back of my knees were sweating?! I did not know this was possible - I felt somewhat jittery as I walked to morning mass - unsure if it was the strange white flag message or the intense high temperatures affecting my poor Scottish body.

I sat on the cool bench of the church and spoke to God as I always did -

Whatever is next for me on my path I will accept - with no resistance whatsoever. The flow of the Universe is always in my favour.

I scurried home desperate to get to my air conditioned apartment and then spent the rest of the day inside, listening to podcasts and watching Graham Norton. It was far too hot to venture out… well until 8pm, when the ice cream shop began calling my name again …

Hazelnut, pistachio and vanilla… I was feeling adventurous. (In case you were wondering)

On Monday the 17th of July I woke early, determined to finish the last of my writing, so that the rest of the week could be spent relaxing, before I would be holidaying for three weeks in the Algarve with Frances. I had arranged to fly back into the UK on the Friday evening, where I would be collecting my little love from her father at Gatwick airport the next morning. Frances and I would then take a short flight later that day, to our favourite part of Portugal.

It was the first few weeks of the summer holidays and I knew my little lady would be super excited for extended beach time and visiting the kids club we had spent so many mornings at, the summer before.

But first - I was planning on relaxing all week to preserve my energy for three weeks of solo parenting.

I wrote all morning and then decided on a whim to have my nails done at the salon right next to my apartment - I had been in the week before and loved the treatments I received, so I made the executive decision to take a break from writing and treat myself one last time before leaving.

As I sat making small talk with the very pretty Spanish nail technician a tall, handsome man walked into the salon and stopped right in front of me. He spoke to me in Spanish and when I hesitated in my reply he repeated his sentence in perfect English.

I own the salon, may I ask if you are happy with the treatments?

I told him yes, his staff were lovely and very good at their jobs, he seemed very pleased with my review and asked me if I needed anything else while I was there

I opened my mouth and the words came out before I knew what I was saying

" I would really like a good steak please, can you help me in providing a recommendation of somewhere in the city"

The man's face lit up as he told me

"You have asked the right person, I am Argentinian - we know our steaks... I will take you to the best steak restaurant in Seville when you are finished here"

For a second I thought he was suggesting he would take me out for lunch - I nodded somewhat reluctantly, confused as to whether I was being asked out on a date.

Least resistance I said to myself, as I sat waiting on my appointment to be over.

And so ten minutes later I was walking through the city centre with this very handsome Argentinian man, asking me lots of questions about my life. When I mentioned my two daughters in the UK .. one of whom is twenty three years old, he immediately showered me with compliments, telling me I did not look old enough to have a daughter that age and he could not believe I had any children at all, as in his words, I had the "perfect figure" … I smiled at the boldness of his words - masculine and direct.

As I walked along I thought about the white flag that was supposedly being waved and wondered if this man, with all his compliments was the personification of the flag. I shook my head in confusion at my own thoughts as I tried my best to keep up with his questions.

But when we got to the restaurant, Alejandro, as I had learned was his name, suddenly shook my hand rather formally, then abruptly turned and walked away.

I walked into the restaurant alone, laughing to myself, thinking … *definitely not taking me out on a date then… definitely not the white flag I've been told to prepare for...*

Steak first perhaps.

When Tim and I were together we had a routine when it came to restaurants - I loved nothing more than sitting down at the table across from him and simply relaxing while taking in the surroundings. I never picked up a menu nor asked for the wine list - Tim always ordered for me - he knew my preferences inside out, so there was never any need for me to read the menu. Our restaurant routine was a symbol of my complete and utter trust in him to make the right decisions for me - in all aspects of our life together. When coaching my female clients in surrender to the masculine (their husbands) this is always the first step I take them through - allowing their husbands to order their food. It is usually met with resistance in the beginning - but my reasoning is this - masculine energy in its highest form is presence

All symbols of the masculine -

Money - all present (even if we have none in the bank it is still present in the world around us at all times)

God - omnipresent- not confined to churches, we can convene with Him at any time or place.

Man - in his highest form, is present and grounded.

I tell my clients - if you allow your husband to be *present* in his masculinity, when he is in the present moment, the one thing he will do, is notice your preferences. He is hardwired to take that information in.

I have never coached a couple where the man has not been able to choose the very thing his wife would have chosen for herself or something that she has said afterwards she enjoyed even more.

How does any woman allow her husband to be present in his masculinity - the easy answer is, she must allow herself to be present in her femininity. The feminine receives from the masculine, this is true both physically in the bedroom, the masculine is emptied and the feminine is filled - and symbolically throughout their lives.

The Masculine provides, the Feminine receives.

The Masculine leads , the Feminine guides.

Letting your man choose for you in a restaurant is symbolic of letting him lead you through life.

Women are hesitant in this part because they are hesitant to surrender and let their man truly lead them in their day to day lives - I go over this in much more detail in my online programme. But for here, see it as the symbol of what it means in the day to day.

Masculine leadership.

During an online group coaching session one day, mixed with both men and women, I explained why I do this, to a business coaching client taking a 'hot seat' on the call with me. If you have never been coached in a group setting before - a hot seat, is an opportunity for a participant to be coached 1-2-1 in the online "room" by the head coach - in this case, me.

The lady I was coaching, had asked a question on burn out, this lead me down the path of asking her how much she allows her husband to lead her *outside* of her business. She immediately remarked on how lovely it would be to be looked after and led in this way. On my screen - I could see many of the men nodding in agreement with what I was saying.These men would love their wives to surrender to their leadership - and they would love to be able to show their devotion to their wives by picking her favourite foods. The masculine wants nothing more than to make the feminine's life easier, to protect and provide. But my words on this were definitely also met with resistance - many women on the call were scornful - one lady wrote to me in the comments - *this is ridiculous, I would never do this - I can make my own decisions on what to order for dinner...*

Scorn is another cover up for fear - why would we feel disdain for something that does not affect us directly?

Anything, and I mean anything, that makes us feel discomfort in our bodies is an indicator of fear. Let's be clear though, fear is necessary, it is a survival technique inherent in every human being, designed to keep us alive. The greatest discernment we can make as humans is understanding when we are *truly* afraid and when our ego is afraid ... anger, scorn, disdain... this is the fear of the ego. A fear of losing the identity that we have created.

I too, can definitely make my own decision on what I would like for dinner. Tim was well aware that I could read and make decisions for myself ... but it was also fun to just relax and have someone else pick for me.

And there I was in Seville, in what was apparently the best steak house in the city, about to read a menu by myself once more. And I felt kinda sad about that in all honesty.

The waiter seemed a little surprised that I was eating alone, but quickly found me a table and brought the menu over - where I was acutely aware that there was no masculine to order for me. And as I sat there looking at the menu I thought again , how it was the little things like this that I missed the most. In truth I loved having Tim order for me in restaurants - I had always loved eating out, ever since I got my first pay check back in the early 2000's and in the recent years with Tim, it added an extra layer of fun waiting to see what would arrive at the table. He would always take his time - making sure to choose exactly the right food for me to enjoy and always managed to pick the perfect wine and dessert too. I had never felt so relaxed as I did eating in restaurants with that man.

But the feminine is nothing if not resourceful - so when the handsome waiter returned I handed him my menu and asked him to bring whatever he recommended for me. I told him how I like my steak but said I would leave the choice completely up to him - adding *I trust you completely* to bolster his confidence, which I could see was a little lacking.

He grinned at my words and nodded enthusiastically.

And *I mean it* I thought in that moment - *I trust the masculine completely.*

It had taken nine months, but my trust in the masculine had returned.

And if I trust the masculine completely - I had to trust that Tim made the right decision in ending our relationship, however much it hurt. I had to surrender to his leadership on *this* matter, just as I had done with everything else in our relationship.

The steak was wonderful, if a little too rare for my liking - but when I mentioned this to my lovely waiter, he promptly whipped my plate away and returned with a brand new one cooked to perfection.

The feminine desires, the masculine makes manifest.

I went back to the apartment, a few hours later, completely satiated and ready to have an early night.

No white flag had been waved as far as I could see, which I could admit to myself, did confuse me slightly. I had become very used to trusting the intelligence of my body, and that message I had received seemed very clear. So I did feel a wave of confusion as the day neared its end.

I lay on the sofa, spent from my time in the sunshine and realised that in the back of my mind, the whole day, I had been expecting something to happen. Now that the day was almost over, with nothing out of the ordinary occurring - other than a very nice steak and a pleasant conversation with a handsome man… I noticed that I felt slightly agitated. My fear was not that there was no white flag - it was that my body had sent a sign I could not decipher, this was the story that was making me feel uncomfortable.

I decided to take myself to the rooftop to watch the sunset and meditate on what I was feeling, in order to let it go. I walked up the two flights of stairs and pushed open the door to the little terrace, the heat although slightly more agreeable, was still intense even at the late hour. The rooftop was empty as usual and I made my way over to a little table and chairs in the corner.

I sat watching the sun set over the many rooftops of Seville and spoke out loud to myself, God and anyone else who was listening... maybe some random Spaniard in the next building...who knows...

Perhaps I am just losing my mind , I very distinctly heard that a white flag would be being waved today - and assumed it would be Tim , but maybe I am just losing my mind in this heat

It is time to move on Aly, it is time , its is time, it is time.

As I said those words, a burst of energy emerged from my chest just like many times over the previous months - releasing the emotion.

I let go.

I had learned all I could learn from this experience. I still had no idea why Tim and I had separated and I had asked God time and time again to show me why - and now I had no other choice, it was time, to just let go and trust.

I thought about the words I had heard repeatedly in my body throughout the previous months -

Who are you? What do you desire? What fears are holding you back ?

Stay Still. Resist Nothing.

I replayed the words over and over and over, rearranging them in my mind -

Accept what is Aly, resist nothing,

Be in the silence

Feel the feelings

I sat there crying for over around an hour in complete surrender, my body shaking violently as I finally let go of trying to control what was happening.

White flag or no white flag - I had been through enough.

I let go of the rope.

That same level of calm detachment was back again.

And it felt good.

I made my way back down to my beautiful apartment, the sun had set - no white flag had been raised and I was at peace with that.

Perhaps my body, which had been speaking to me louder and louder in the months that preceded this message, had picked up a signal meant for someone else. Perhaps the white flag was mine to be waved to myself - so many possibilities … but none of them mattered.

I laughed as I watched my ego make a last ditch attempt to hold on - to question the wisdom of my body instead of just accepting it

nope Aly, no more questions, let go.

I took my journal out from the drawer on the bedside table and began writing

'It's been exactly 40 weeks since the day my life came crashing down around my ears.

40 weeks - the gestational period for the birth of new life

A version of me died, 40 weeks ago from today and it has taken nine long months to rebirth this new version who sits here this evening…

I feel peace in my body unlike anything I have ever felt before.'

I hadn't noticed how dark the apartment had become since I came down from the rooftop. With just the light from the ensuite, left on absentmindedly earlier that day, providing just enough illumination into the room to allow me to complete my journal.

As I stretched and stood to get ready for bed I remembered my mobile phone, still in my bag where I left it earlier in the evening.

I made a vow to myself there and then - *no more sleeping late, tomorrow I will set my alarm and start my day early … my new life is out there waiting to be grabbed with both hands. I must not sleep in for it - we begin tomorrow …*

I smiled, a warm genuine smile to myself , truly excited for the amazing life ahead of me - starting the very next day with a walk in the morning sun, obviously super early before the intense heat took over!

On a whim I grabbed a pen and wrote on my white board paper hanging on the wall of the kitchen, my intentions for the week and the month ahead:

Success with my book launch
Happy times in Aljezur with Frances
LOVE!!!!
Someone to open my jar of pickled onions :)

I had been trying to open that damn jar for three days, to no avail. I pictured myself, the next morning, a damsel in distress, out on the streets of Seville, jar of pickles in hand looking for a knight in shining armour to help me , the knight arriving …

waving a white flag of course

My imagination knows no limits

Still laughing at my own thoughts - I retrieved my phone to set an alarm for the next day.

The screen lit up - a familiar name, with a short, direct message, sent an hour before, while I had been sitting on the rooftop talking to God.

"Aly … when are you back in the UK .. I want to speak with you, in person"

A white flag … just like my body had told me.

The body knows the way.

Always.

My body spoke again in that moment

Least resistance …

And I knew then, that my new way of living was about to be put to the test, more than it ever had before.

The question was - did I really have the courage to follow the Path of Least Resistance?

I was about to find out…..

EPILOGUE

It is not what matters to you - but how you tell the story.

My life has always been a story of paradox.

I grew up in a town in Scotland that was riddled with addiction and poverty, unemployment levels were high, expectations were low - but the scenery, the hills and lochs, are amongst the most beautiful you will ever see. The people, my God, the people there would give you the coat off their back to keep you warm. Everyone is welcomed, everyone is loved.

I grew up in a house where I was sexually abused as a ten year old girl- but the fun and laughter we had amongst us five children, shaped me into the woman I am today. Quick witted, full of sarcasm and silliness, these are the traits I have decided to keep.

I grew up with a mother who taught me how to be a people pleaser, stoic, distracted, lacking in boundaries … but she also taught me kindness, how to see the best in others, how to forgive.

We live in a world of paradox - everything has an opposite.

Energy is created within polarity.

We cannot have the masculine without the feminine, and vice versa - and the divine child born of these two energies is the key to our golden ticket life.

I used to think terms like golden ticket life, spiritual awakening, personal journey, higher self etc were, well, for want of a better word - a bit wanky … a bit pretentious. I had no idea what they really meant to be honest - they were not phrases or words we used in our house growing up.

And that's when I realised I felt uncomfortable because I had never had any experience of using them - it was just fear, dressed up in discomfort.

It's always just fear - dressed up in stories.

I felt a bit embarrassed saying out loud, in therapy, that I could hear a Voice inside of me that seemed to be guiding me onto the right path … *im not sure if its even a Voice , its more of a feeling. But its clear and concise and if I don't follow it, shit hits the fan. So I've just been following it.. is this normal?*

Ed, one of the two amazing men (Tim being the other one) who initiated me into healing - was delighted when I told him this - he told me time and time again:

Trust the Voice within Aly

(I capitalise the word Voice, to give it the importance it deserves, it is the Voice of God after all)

And so I began to trust it - no matter what it said. I learned to ask my body when the fears in my mind caused me to falter. My body always answered clearly and concisely - there was never any hesitation - just do this, dont do that.

Clear messages such as :

Stay still. Stand up. Be seen. Raise your voice. Tell the women.

I knew then I had to teach my clients how to trust their internal Voice - how to trust their bodies again.

The wonderful women in my group kept asking me - *is this real Aly, this magic inside of me?*

Yes, its real - its very, very real.

Women's bodies are magical (listen, I love the men folk, and in the past have coached hundreds of men, but these days I am all about showing the women the magic they hold within)

There is an intelligence inside the bodies of women that is being distracted from more and more with every passing generation

We are dwindling in numbers - the healers, the seers, the wise women. We have more distraction techniques than ever before (hello, social media?) We are constantly being encouraged and conditioned to look *out there* instead of inwards - into where the magic is.

The magic is not out there - it never has been. It never will be.

The magic, the intuition, the sheer *knowing* - it is carried inside the body of every woman walking this planet.

And the thing is, we know its there - its like an itch we cannot scratch, a constant tapping on the shoulder -it is telling us - it does not have to be this way, it is asking us to listen.

That is why we distract ourselves, the tapping on the shoulder is trying to tell us we are destined for *more* - more feeling, more wildness… *more magic*. And that feels big and powerul and magical and a little scary, of course. But we know what is on the other side of fear.

The feminine creates - the masculine makes manifest in the world of matter.

The masculine (both within us and in the form of our partner) makes manifest with *action* (or inaction in a lot of cases, action can also mean inaction - doing by *not* doing, especially if you have spent much of your life doing)

The feminine creates from the subconscious

We are literally creating our own realities around us in every given moment.

If life doesn't feel good right now - that is of our creation - we are both the problem and the solution. This is not blame or judgement - it is responsibility and sheer power.

When we recognise how powerful we are we can begin to write a new story.

We hold the Golden Ticket in our hand - the path to that big dream life - ***we are the Path,*** our energy is creating it, literally as we walk along.

But that energy must be clear or the path will be difficult.

The Path of Least Resistance is the easiest, clearest path.

I promise you this - because I have walked it for the past year - I continue to walk it daily.

What are you resisting in your life right now? What do you most dislike about your current life situation?

Write it down.

Then go look in the mirror - you are creating this life, you and only you can change it.

You have that power! Isn't that amazing?

What is the next step to change?

Don't tell me how someone else has to do something for your life to change, or how a situation has to occur for the next step to be taken.

Tell me how *you* have the *power* to create.

Don't look out there - out there does not exist.

The only reality we have is the one we have created in our own minds.

Don't blame other people for the things you are unhappy about in your current reality- you are putting your power in someone else's hands.

That power belongs to you - it is your birthright.

I coach women on their relationships, but we start with the relationship they have with *themselves* first and foremost .Only then do we look at the relationship they have with their partner.

This is difficult for the women when they first come to work with me. They want to look at their husbands, they want someone else *out there* to come and rescue them. They want to place their unhappiness in someone else's hands. The first thing I tell them is - we don't do that around here. We don't give the power of our own happiness to anyone or anything, not our husbands, our children - or our careers.

We are not damsels in distress, we never have been (unless its with a jar of pickled onions, then we can be the damsel in distress)

I tell my clients every single day -

stop looking at him and go look in the mirror

They arrive in front of me full of stories :

"I just don't know if my husband can step up to the plate" … what plate? The high expectation plate you created in your own mind? Have you stepped up to it? Put the plate down … stop looking at him and go look in the mirror.

"he isn't masculine enough" … who holds the yardstick for masculinity? You? Ok, but - are you feminine "enough"? Stop looking at him and go look in the mirror

"I'm tired, I want him to do more for me" …. Let's turn that around, lady - *I* want to do more for me, by doing *less*, I'm tired of doing it all… stop looking at him and go look in the mirror.

You have the power - you have always had the power.

I say this to my clients with the most love in my heart - I am not suggesting their husbands are perfect beings, who never do any wrong - but their perception of what is *actually* happening is almost always skewed by the emotions they have repressed inside from long, long ago.

(Of course there have been times when relationships have just run their course, incompatibilities have been discovered and the natural flow of the Universe opens up a new path. When women learn to really trust their bodies for the first time, sometimes they realise their new path may involve a very different life)

But for the most part -the one thing that comes up again and again, is usually - *Aly, I just don't know if i can trust him ...*

And the truth is , we don't trust ourselves, we dont trust that our *body* chose the right mate - because we disassociated from it at a very young age.

This is not our fault - this was due to not having a safe environment to feel our feelings.

Now we know what the problem is, this can be rectified ... we can go back into the body and learn to feel the feelings.

Breathwork, meditation, menstruation, orgasm - the modalities we use.

The body knows who you are.
The body knows what you desire .
The body knows your fears are not real.

My friend Acacia calls me the mean coach, jokingly ... kinda - I don't placate my clients, I tell them how it is, I show them their blind spots. It can be difficult to hear.

I don't do it to judge or shame, I do it simply to remind them of their power. I want all women to remember their power.

A woman *relaxed in her body* can change her entire world.

Women hold more power within ourselves than we know what do with - this is why we need the men, to pull us back down to earth when we fly off in our magical worlds.

I don't say anything to my clients that I haven't already said to myself, a million times over in a million different ways.

Tim waved the white flag, in July last year, just like my body told me he would.

I did not resist what the Universe placed on my path. I stayed open, I listened to my body.

I sit here today, writing this, with six months of the ultimate Least Resistance in the bag.

Friends, I have to tell you - at times, is has been excruciatingly painful - surrendering to the man who broke my heart, who threw me headfirst down a spiral of despair with one sentence

This isn't going to feel good, Aly

He was damn right , it did not *feel* good.

But I felt the feelings - all the feelings. And I have Tim to thank for that.

How I choose to see what happened in the nine months we were apart, is the power I hold within myself. I choose to see the lessons I learned, the strength I gained and the story I have to tell.

I chose to thank Tim for the decision he made - because it changed my life. He gave me exactly what I needed - a chance to see myself, to choose myself, to know myself... to FEEL myself.

I know who I am.

I know what I desire.

I know that when the fears arise, as they sometimes still do, they are not real.

I choose to listen to the wisdom of my body.

All magical, all sensual, all feeling ... all knowing.

This is the way of the women.

I spent much of my life pretending to be someone else, an avatar I had created as a little girl, terrifed of anyone seeing the real me. And then, one day, I gently took the pen out of the hands of a ten year old child and began rewriting my story.

Our story.

I am creating that story in the *present* with the flow of the Universe and the spiritual wisdom of my body.

Resisting nothing ...

Gaining everything.

ΔΔΔ

If you have enjoyed reading my ramblings and would like to learn more about the methods I used (and continue to use) to clear my energetic body of a lifetime of repressed emotions - I invite you to join the waiting list for my self study programme coming this year:

The Way of The Women.

This nine week self paced digital programme contains in -depth guidance on using my 4 Elements of breathwork, meditation, menstruation & orgasm to get you back in touch with the magical wisdom of your body.

Please visit:

leastresistance.life/thewayofthewomen

for more information and to join the waiting list.

Thank you.

Printed in Great Britain
by Amazon

40290825R00067